EASTERN
MASSACHUSETTS

OTHER BOOKS FROM BRIGHT LEAF

House Stories
*The Meanings of Home
in a New England Town*
BETH LUEY

Bricklayer Bill
*The Untold Story of
the Workingman's Boston Marathon*
PATRICK L. KENNEDY AND
LAWRENCE W. KENNEDY

Concrete Changes
*Architecture, Politics, and the
Design of Boston City Hall*
BRIAN M. SIRMAN

Williamstown and Williams College
Explorations in Local History
DUSTIN GRIFFIN

Massachusetts Treasures
A Guide to Marvelous, Must-See Museums
CHUCK D'IMPERIO

Boston's Twentieth-Century Bicycling
Renaissance
Cultural Change on Two Wheels
LORENZ J. FINISON

Went to the Devil
A Yankee Whaler in the Slave Trade
ANTHONY J. CONNORS

At Home
Historic Houses of Eastern Massachusetts
BETH LUEY

Black Lives, Native Lands,
White Worlds
A History of Slavery in New England
JARED ROSS HARDESTY

At Home
*Historic Houses of Central and
Western Massachusetts*
BETH LUEY

Flight Calls
Exploring Massachusetts through Birds
JOHN R. NELSON

Lost Wonderland
*The Brief and Brilliant Life of Boston's
Million Dollar Amusement Park*
STEPHEN R. WILK

Legends of the Common Stream
JOHN HANSON MITCHELL

I Believe I'll Go Back Home
*Roots and Revival in
New England Folk Music*
THOMAS S. CURREN

Minds and Hearts
*The Story of James Otis Jr.
and Mercy Otis Warren*
JEFFREY H. HACKER

Letters from Red Farm
*The Untold Story of the Friendship
between Helen Keller and Journalist
Joseph Edgar Chamberlin*
ELIZABETH EMERSON

The Combat Zone
*Murder, Race, and Boston's
Struggle for Justice*
JAN BROGAN

Bright Leaf | Amherst and Boston
An imprint of University of Massachusetts Press

TRAIL

BEN KIMBALL

RUNNING

EASTERN
MASSACHUSETTS

Trail Running Eastern Massachusetts has been supported by the Regional Books Fund, established by donors in 2019 to support the University of Massachusetts Press's Bright Leaf imprint.

Bright Leaf, an imprint of the University of Massachusetts Press, publishes accessible and entertaining books about New England. Highlighting the history, culture, diversity, and environment of the region, Bright Leaf offers readers the tools and inspiration to explore its landmarks and traditions, famous personalities, and distinctive flora and fauna.

ISBN 978-1-62534-635-3 (paper)

Designed by Deste Roosa
Set in Quadraat and Calluna Sans
Printed and bound by Books International, Inc.

Cover design by Deste Roosa
Cover photo by Ben Kimball, Three women running along a scenic trail in eastern Massachusetts, 2021. Courtesy of the photographer.

Library of Congress Cataloging-in-Publication Data
A catalog record for this book is available from the Library of Congress.

British Library Cataloguing-in-Publication Data
A catalog record for this book is available from the British Library.

Portions of the introduction were previously published in Trail Running Western Massachusetts (Lebanon, NH: University Press of New England, 2015). Copyright © 2015 University Press of New England.

PAGE i Trail racing at Callahan State Park in Framingham.
PAGE iii Inviting trail curve at Groton Town Forest.
PAGES x–xi Quabbin Reservoir vista from Soapstone Hill in Petersham.

All photos and maps by Ben Kimball.

Contents

Acknowledgments

This guide was created with the support and assistance of countless friends in the regional running community. First, my awesome partner, Jennifer Garrett, once again helped with everything, including GPS work, editing, and logistics, not to mention endless encouragement. Others who provided invaluable advice, insight, or company include Pete and Tara Abele, Rufus Chaffee, Jason Como, Tom Davidson, Micah Donahue, Bob Fitzgerald, Brenda Fortin, Chase Fuller, Chris Gaughan, Paul Jahnige, Jay Kelly, Lydia Kimball, Orin Parvin, Amy Rusiecki, Jason Sarouhan, Tom Van den Broeck Raffensperger, Jesse Veinotte, Anne Marie Winchester, and Chris Wristen. Special thanks to Síofra Cléirigh Büttner, Katrina Coogan, and Jennifer Garrett for their positive energy and high spirits on a hot day during the cover photo shoot. Many organizations and resources proved useful for researching trails, including Massachusetts Department of Conservation and Recreation (DCR), the Trustees, various land trusts and conservation groups, and several online mapping sites. All profiled routes were visited and mapped in person, however, and any errors in them are entirely my own. Most of the base-map layers and some of the connecting trails data were obtained from MassGIS and various municipalities. Thanks also to the terrific production staff at UMass Press; they ensured every stage of this project ran very smoothly. Finally, special thanks to the local conservation organizations, land trusts, recreation departments, hiking clubs, trail running clubs (particularly TARC), mountain bike clubs (particularly NEMBA), friends groups, and volunteers who help build and maintain the wonderful trails of eastern and central Massachusetts.

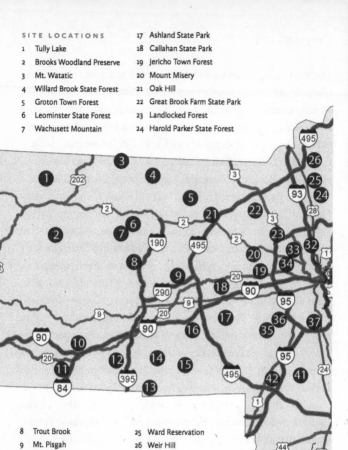

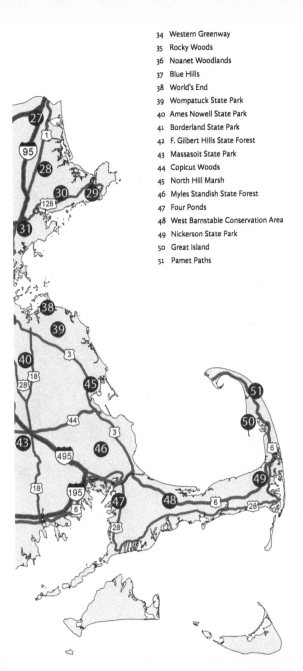

TRAIL
RUNNING
EASTERN
MASSACHUSETTS

Introduction

Whether swiftly gliding through the woods, leaping over fallen logs, or soaring along scenic mountain ridges, trail runners always seem to be enjoying themselves. This is hardly surprising, since trail running combines the best aspects of many healthy and enjoyable activities. Among other things, it provides opportunities for achieving good fitness workouts, spending time outdoors exploring new terrain, and connecting to the natural landscape in a direct and personal way. The appeal of trail racing has become apparent to the broader running community, and the sport remains extremely popular.

Trail running is a particularly tactile experience, constantly forcing you to be mindful and aware of the world around you. Since it frequently requires the body to balance and stabilize itself, it strengthens different sets of muscles than running on pavement and generally results in less impact on the legs. No special gear is needed, though trail-running shoes improve grip and comfort in various conditions such as mud, grass, and loose rocks; handheld water bottles or hydration packs can be very helpful on longer runs; and traction is useful in winter.

Hiking is often an integral part of trail running, especially on steep slopes, but (pro) you can cover more miles in less time and (con) potentially move more quickly past sights. You also feel the ground differently—flowing over it rather than just stepping on it—and you make crucial, split-second decisions about where to place your feet with each stride.

EASTERN MASSACHUSETTS TRAIL SITES Eastern Massachusetts offers an incredible number of great trail-running opportunities, from out-and-back runs on popular long-distance routes, such as the Midstate Trail and the Bay Circuit Trail, to little-known loops hidden away in the woods. Though many areas are heavily populated, with urban and suburban development limiting the number of options available, particularly close to the sizable cities, you can still find plenty of places where runners can roam for miles.

The intent of this guide is to present a diverse selection of enjoyable runs in the region. While featuring many sites for experienced runners seeking less traveled but still interesting and fun trails away from the beaten path, it also aims to be inclusive, with a number of easily accessible sites for anyone looking for first-step exposure to trail running. However, it generally avoids short paths at smaller sites, loops shorter than three miles, and paved or partly paved pathways. Naturally, there are hundreds more sites where you can find good local trail-running options if you do multiple loops on shorter trails or link smaller sites together. Local schools often have great cross-country trail networks nearby, too.

Geographically, the book covers the area between Quabbin Reservoir and the coast, including Cape Cod (the islands, which require ferries to reach, are also covered in a section at the end). Elevations range from sea level to the top of Wachusett Mountain. The trails profiled also represent a range of difficulty levels and terrain types. Other factors considered in final site selection included access, current condition, and adequate parking.

There are options here for everyone. However, these are still only a sampling; there are *many* other trails out there to explore—including some more great ones just waiting for you to discover them. Make sure to check each site's "Nearby" section for a few ideas.

LONG-DISTANCE TRAILS AND RAIL TRAILS While this book specifically profiles fifty-one of the best trail-running sites in eastern Massachusetts, other good options can be found along almost any portion of the region's most prominent long-distance routes, like the Bay Circuit Trail (about 200 miles; not completely contiguous, with some short road sections), the Midstate Trail (92 contiguous miles), and the Boroughs Loop Trail (33 miles; some road). For example, in addition to the sections described at Mt. Watatic, Wachusett Mountain, and

Douglas State Forest, numerous point-to-point or out-and-back runs are possible along the Midstate Trail at sites like Barre Falls Dam, Savage Hill Wildlife Management Area, Oakham State Forest, Sibley Farm, Hodges Village Dam, and Moose Hill WMA. Official websites offer detailed maps and information.

Likewise, the region's many unpaved rail-trail corridors can be accessed from myriad locations and offer endless easy running routes that are especially good for beginner trail runners or anyone just looking for gentle out-and-back runs on flat dirt surfaces; these include the Mass Central Rail Trail, Border-to-Boston Trail, Marblehead Rail Trail, Wenham Canal Trail, Grand Trunk Trail / Titanic Rail Trail, Quinebaug River Rail Trail, Upper Charles Rail Trail, Ware River Rail Trail, and Southern New England Trunkline Trail, among others. Note that portions of some rail trails are in the process of being paved. The mostly dirt paths flanking the Charles River in Cambridge/ Boston could also be considered a distinctly metropolitan but still very scenic trail run.

CONSERVATION Trail running's continued rise in popularity brings increased environmental impact on the beautiful pathways and landscapes we all love to escape to. By promoting and practicing low-impact mindsets and suggesting best practices for treading lightly, we can try to preserve these treasured resources for generations to come.

Avoid running on trails when they're most vulnerable, particularly in spring. As the snow melts from a long New England winter, everyone wants to get out and hit the trails; unfortunately, this is when the impact from running can do the most damage. Ground saturated with snowmelt is soft and easily eroded, and formerly pleasant paths can quickly become ruts of exposed roots and rocks. Staying off the trails during the wettest weeks will help ensure that they remain in top shape for the rest of the year. It's also preferable to stick to the middle of existing trails—even if that means encountering a mud puddle or two—rather than going off to the side, which widens trails and unnecessarily hastens erosion. Finally, *never* cut off a switchback in the trail; they're there specifically to lessen the grade and prevent erosion.

Dispersing is another way to reduce impact. Instead of always visiting a favorite popular trail, consider going to such places only on weekdays when crowds are smaller and using your weekends to explore more remote, less visited sites. Not only will you decrease use at the popular site, you may also find greater solitude, have a more pleasant experience, and increase your appreciation for the natural diversity of the region.

Perhaps most important, you can get involved with conservation organizations that are committed to preserving and maintaining stewardship over natural areas and publicly accessible lands with trails. In eastern Massachusetts, there are many excellent local land trusts and "friends" groups you can support with financial pledges or service hours; a lot of them host volunteer maintenance workdays where you can help out and keep the trails in top condition.

ETIQUETTE Observing several basic rules of behavior will go a long way toward fostering goodwill with landowners and land managers and helping to ensure continued public access to a wide variety of trails. The more we present a positive image of runners as respectful and responsible users of trails, the better an experience everyone will have and the more welcome we'll be in the future.

Encounters with other users are virtually guaranteed, even at the remotest of sites. Always be courteous of hikers, bikers, and other runners, making way whenever possible. Also, never underestimate the powerful good vibes that can be generated by a simple "hello" or friendly nod to a fellow trail user. If you encounter a motorized off-road vehicle such as an all-terrain vehicle or motorbike, you as a pedestrian have the right-of-way—technically. But demonstrate kindness and step aside for them anyway, especially on any trails specifically designated for their use; you will likely hear them long before they see you anyway.

Mountain bikes are allowed at most sites unless otherwise noted, though some trails are posted as off-limits. Likewise, dogs are allowed at many sites; exceptions are indicated in the text. Dogs should always be leashed (except in designated areas), but don't count on their owners always leashing them.

Finally, bear in mind that while many trail networks (such as those in state parks and forests) were designed for a variety of recreational uses, others specifically encourage quiet and passive uses. For example, running is often specifically prohibited on trails at most Mass Audubon properties and many wildlife sanctuaries; for that reason, few are included here. Town parks designated for "residents only" are also excluded. At properties where running is allowed but the primary purpose is conservation, please take extra care to not disturb wildlife or native vegetation, or other visitors who are there specifically to enjoy those things.

SAFETY While there are a number of factors to consider when planning a trail run, none is more important than hydration: you simply have to have enough water. There are dozens of handheld water bottles and hydration packs on the market in which you can carry water, sports drinks, whatever. Experiment with what works best for you; just make sure you drink. One note of caution: never drink untreated water from an untested source.

Insects are probably the most common animals you'll encounter. Extra clothing or bug repellent deters mosquitoes and blackflies, which can be maddening in large numbers, especially in the days following summer rainstorms. Tick checks are a must after any run through shrubby or grassy areas. Wasps, hornets, and yellowjackets may also be encountered. Your best defense against them is to be on the lookout for nests, but should you accidentally stir some up or find yourself getting stung, just do what comes naturally: run away as fast as you can.

Encounters with large mammals are rare, but you may see deer or black bears. A black bear will typically run away should you happen upon one, but if it doesn't, back away and leave it be if possible or make noise and try to look big if it appears threatening. In more remote areas, you might see a moose. Moose rarely charge, but it's best to stay out of their way and observe from a distance, just in case. Note that seasonal hunting is permitted on many of the properties profiled in this book. For up-to-date hunting-season information, check with the Massachusetts Department of Fish & Game, and if you'll be running during an open season, wear bright-orange clothing.

Naturally, trail runners must take care to avoid falls and physical injuries such as sprained ankles while out in the woods. Potential hazards to watch out for include wet rocks or ledges, slopes covered in loose gravel, and wet or slippery leaves. Practicing mindfulness and slowing your pace appropriately while making your way along a rough section of trail are necessary to ensure safe foot placement as you travel over the constantly changing terrain.

Trail runners should also be aware of poison ivy; make sure you know what it looks like and where it tends to grow. Poison ivy often thrives in disturbed areas and can be particularly dense right along the edges of roads, trails, and rivers, especially at lower elevations. Usually you can step over or pick your way through a patch along a trail, but a slight detour may be called for on occasion.

Always leave early enough in the day to make it back to the trailhead by nightfall, unless you plan to run with a headlamp. Also, check the weather forecast before heading out, particularly for remote sites or if taking trails that ascend to higher elevations. Prepare for the worst conditions possible and be willing to change your plans based on changes in the weather—even if it means cutting your run short. When it's wet and chilly out, be watchful for any early warning signs of hypothermia, such as cold feet and hands, pale skin, shivering, fatigue, or slurred speech. Hypothermia can be especially dangerous in temperatures just above freezing. Lastly, consider telling someone your intended route and an estimated return time.

TRAIL ACCESS All the trails profiled in this guide are open to the public. Most are on public or publicly accessible land, but occasional portions cross privately owned parcels. This is especially true of long-distance trails like the Bay Circuit Trail and the Midstate Trail. When following publicly accessible trails that cross private property, always respect the rights and desires of the landowners. Obey all posted notices, especially any "No Trespassing" signs, and never intentionally move or damage structures such as fences or gates. Only currently open trails were included at the time of this guide's writing, but users should be aware that trail closures or reroutings (or both) are possible at any time.

HOW TO USE THIS BOOK Each trail-running route in this book has a chapter dedicated to it, as numbered on the locator map. Each site profile begins with quick-reference data for easily determining if it's suitable for your running ambitions on a given day, including:

Distance Total mileage of the suggested route

Town Municipality(s) the site is in

Difficulty Rating Subjective categories of easy, moderate, and challenging (or combinations)

Trail Style Shape of the route on a map, including loop, lollipop (a loop with a "stick" portion), out-and-back, and figure-8

Trail Type Width and character of the trail itself; includes singletrack, doubletrack, and dirt road

Total Ascent Cumulative elevation gain (best estimation) of the entire primary suggested route

This basic data is followed by a general description of that profile's route, highlighting some of the standout features you'll encounter there. Next comes directions to the trailhead from the nearest town or highway and GPS search suggestions.

The bulk of each chapter is given over to detailed, sometimes turn-by-turn trail descriptions of the route itself that—along with a judicious use of the maps contained in this book—should get you from start to finish without making a wrong turn or becoming mystifyingly lost in the wilderness. These sections often include optional extensions for lengthening a given run or—alternatively—trims for shortening if you don't want to tackle the entire trail that day.

Finally, each site profile spotlights other *nearby* sites that are good for trail running (there are a lot more than fifty-one!).

TERMINOLOGY Trail running uses some descriptive lingo that general readers (and some runners) may not be familiar with. The following frequently used terms appear throughout the profiles:

4-way intersection A crossing of two trails
Bootleg trail An unofficial trail or faint "trace" path
Braid When a trail splits then later comes back together
Doubletrack A trail wide enough for two people side-by-side
Fork Like a Y-junction, only with two of the trails tighter together
Lollipop loop Loop route that starts/ends with an out-and-back stem
Runnable A highly subjective term indicating "not too steep or rough"
Saddle Low point or notch between two summits
Singletrack A trail wide enough for one person
Switchback A tight S or Z where the trail changes direction on an
    ascent or descent
Technical A trail with more rocks and roots than dirt, often with steep
    pitches
T-junction When one trail ends at another; perpendicular to it
Woods road/dirt road Similar to doubletrack, but slightly wider
Y-junction A 3-way intersection, often with equal angles

DISTANCE 4.4 Miles   **TOWN** Royalston
DIFFICULTY RATING Moderate   **TRAIL STYLE** Loop
TRAIL TYPE Singletrack   **TOTAL ASCENT** 270 Feet

Arguably straddling the border between eastern and western Massachusetts in the North Quabbin region, Tully Lake is definitely a top trail-running site for the state. The Lake Trail (a.k.a. the Tully Lake Loop Trail) is a spectacularly scenic route featuring lakeside views, lovely streams, forested hillsides, and a roaring waterfall. The loop is well marked with blue blazes and makes a terrific trail run for athletes of any ability. Though this site is frequently crowded on weekends, it's generally only lightly visited otherwise. Tully Lake is part of a U.S. Army Corps of Engineers flood-control project, and portions may be flooded in early spring; check with the Trustees, who run the lake's campground, or ACOE for current conditions. The bugs are notoriously brutal at times, and you may want to bring a head net or fly patches in midsummer.

DIRECTIONS From Athol, take Rte. 32 north for 4 miles to Tully Dam, where there are paved parking lots on both sides of the street. It's also possible to park at and start this loop from the boat ramp just north of the dam, Tully Lake Campground north of the lake, or the Doane's Falls trailhead above the northeast side of the lake.
GPS "Tully Lake Disc Golf Course"

TRAIL At the parking area on the south end of Tully Dam, look for the trailhead kiosk. Following the blue-blazed Lake Trail into the woods, take an immediate left and pass the first tee of the disc golf course, then drop down the hill through the trees. At the bottom, veer left

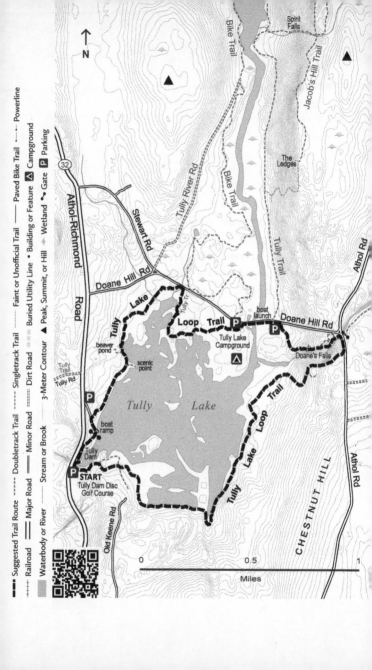

and cross an open field. The trail briefly follows an old road, passes tee 2, crosses the broken pavement of another old road, and passes by several more disc-golf tees.

For a mile and a half, gently wind through the woods along the south and east shores of the lake; much of it is very runnable. The surface is soft and smooth most of the way, with occasional rocks and roots. Several stream crossings may be difficult in spring or after rain events, but they're easily manageable during drier times.

About 2 miles from the start, swing right, away from the lake, and begin climbing at an easy, then moderate, grade on a doubletrack path. At a signed curve where the wide path swings right, bear left onto singletrack again and then ascend at a moderate grade to Athol Road. Turn left and briefly follow the pavement shoulder downhill and across the bridge over Lawrence Brook to the small upper parking lot for Doane's Falls. Just past the bridge, turn left and descend the trail to Doane's Falls. This series of cascades is one of the state's more spectacular waterfalls when water levels are high. Keep following the trail down the steep slope below the falls, then veer right and arrive at the lower parking area.

Go left on Doane Hill Road, following blue-blazed posts and crossing over Tully River, to Tully Lake Campground on the left. The trail reenters the woods at a sign near the parking lot. Follow the rolling trail through the woods along the edge of the lake. Several side spurs lead left to open lakeside views along this pretty peninsula. The main trail veers sharply left just before reaching the road again and then traces the northwest shore of the lake for about a mile to the boat launch; this section can be somewhat rough due to rocks, roots, and muddy stream crossings, but it becomes gentler as you approach the well-used picnic area. Look for short side trails up to a beaver pond and down to a scenic point on the lake.

At the boat launch, briefly follow the paved ramp left down toward the water, then bear right and head up into an open grassy field at a yellow gate. This part is lightly marked; look for a blue-blazed wooden post out in the open. Follow the path toward the stony dam. About halfway up the slope (depending on water levels), the path traverses the side of the dam. Just before the fenced-off spillway, turn sharply right and climb the concrete steps to the parking lot.

Optional Extension The northern half of the Lake Trail is also part of the 22-mile Tully Trail, a remote loop that visits several major waterfalls and open ledges with sweeping scenic vistas (including Tully Mountain and Jacob's Hill). Tully Trail makes a challenging but rewarding long trail run, best attempted in dry conditions and when there's a breeze so the bugs aren't too bad. It's blazed with yellow rectangles the entire way, though the far northern part briefly coincides with the white-blazed New England Trail (NET).

A 7.5-mile loop can be made by running just the eastern portion of the Tully Loop counterclockwise, then returning to the lake and campground via a route that traces the western edge of Tully River below Davis Hill. Marked with orange blazes, the "Bike Trail" gently flows along the edge of the wetland, occasionally following the forested tops of winding natural eskers. It is absolutely delightful for running; there are some short technical sections, but most is smooth and easy.

NEARBY Other good trails in the area can be found at **Royalston Falls** along the northern side of the **Tully Trail** where the NET enters New Hampshire (look for an easy-to-miss natural stone arch near the stream just south of the state line) and at **Jacob's Hill** and **Spirit Falls** along the northeast side of the Tully Trail. The **Bearsden Forest Conservation Area** about 5 miles southeast of Tully Lake features over ten miles of challenging trails and dirt roads that roam over steeply rolling hills, pass by scenic ponds, and delve into deep river gorges. Runners seeking mostly flat doubletrack trails and remote dirt roads will find plenty to enjoy about 10 miles to the east at **Otter River State Forest** in Baldwinville.

Doane's Falls in Royalston.

Tully Lake in Athol.

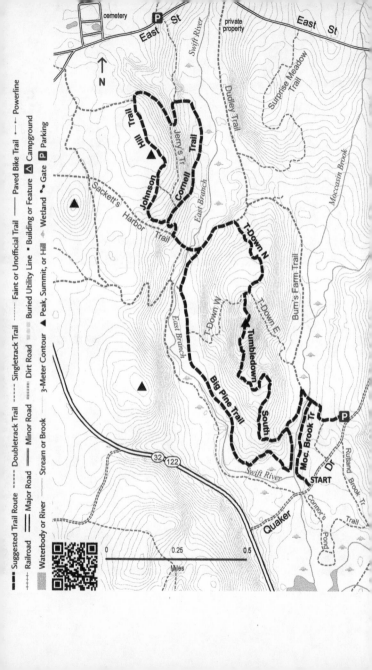

DISTANCE 4.7 Miles   **TOWN** Petersham
DIFFICULTY RATING Easy/Moderate   **TRAIL STYLE** Figure-8 Loop
TRAIL TYPE Singletrack/Doubletrack   **TOTAL ASCENT** 440 Feet

The Brooks Woodland Preserve, or Brooks Preserve, forms the core of a system of adjacent conserved lands with trails, including North Common Meadows, Harvard Forest, Swift River Reservation, and Rutland Brook Wildlife Sanctuary. Much of the landscape consists of forests regrown from former fields and pastures, as evidenced by the many stone walls and old cellar holes. The trails comprise a collection of old woods roads, doubletrack trails, and singletrack footpaths. The suggested route forms a figure-8 loop utilizing a variety of trail types (particularly fun ones to run) and visits many features on the property. This site can also be accessed from a small pull-off along the north side of East Street.

DIRECTIONS From Petersham, go 1.5 miles southeast on Rte. 122. Turn left onto Quaker Drive (a dirt road; may be closed in winter), and go 0.4 miles north to a small dirt parking lot on the left, marked by a Trustees sign. Quaker Drive is about 6 miles northwest of Barre on the right side of Rte. 122.
GPS   "Brooks Woodland Preserve, Quaker Drive"

TRAIL Follow Quaker Drive south down the hill for about 0.2 miles. Just before a small bridge, take a right and head into the woods on Moccasin Brook Trail. This singletrack path follows the east bank of a brook for about a quarter of a mile north to a T-junction with Burn's Farm Trail. There are rocks and roots along this short section, but it's very scenic.

Take a left on the wide doubletrack of Burn's Farm Trail. Immediately cross Moccasin Brook on a bridge and climb gently to a T-junction with the Yellow Loop trail. At the junction, go left on the yellow-blazed Big Pine Trail. Follow this wide, rolling doubletrack trail, initially south along Moccasin Brook and then north along the East Branch of the Swift River (the largest tributary of the Quabbin Reservoir); along this gently undulating trail you'll pass signed junctions with Tumbledown South and West Trails on the right. Also pass an unmarked path leading to a ford of the stream on the left.

At a T-junction, take a left and immediately cross a wooden bridge over the river, then climb a short distance to another junction. Turn right and follow the light-blue-blazed Cornell Trail north, staying right at the first junction. After rolling along for a quarter mile or so, swing left and climb to a Y-junction.

Optional Extension From here you can go north to the network of loop trails at North Common Meadow. The trails there are almost all rugged doubletrack and can be a bit sloppy when wet, especially around and in the meadow, but they're all runnable. Tip: Ledges Trail isn't quite as interesting as it sounds; the outer perimeter loop along Buttercup might make for a better run.

From the junction, stay on the blue-blazed trail and climb the slope, passing Jerry's Trail on the left. You'll soon arrive at a stone memorial bench on the left. Keep climbing to a Y-junction where the grade levels off. Turn left onto Johnson Hill Trail and follow it south across and then down the hill. Drop steeply back to the Cornell Trail, passing several junctions with Jerry's Trail on the left. At the cellar holes, turn right then take an immediate left. Recross the bridge over the river and arrive back at the Yellow Loop. Go left and climb gently to a T-junction.

Turn right on the white-dot-blazed Tumbledown North trail and climb at a moderate grade, passing back and forth through old stone walls. Go right at an unmarked junction with the upper end of Tumbledown East, then take an immediate left on Tumbledown South (Tumbledown West goes straight). You'll soon arrive at the top of the hill where there's a (winter-only) view to the east.

From the vista, head downhill on Tumbledown South. This winding path descends the south side of the hill past stone walls and large boulders. The footing is excellent, and it's really fun to run. At the bottom, veer left back onto the Yellow Loop. At the next junction, turn right, recross the bridge over Moccasin Brook, and go straight ahead up to an open meadow. The path winds through the field and then reaches a T-junction. Turn left and climb a short distance back to the parking lot.

NEARBY While running is discouraged at Mass Audubon's Rutland Brook Wildlife Sanctuary, the main trail is well worth a hike; access via either the Rutland Brook or Connor's Pond Trail. There are several shorter loops just to the south at the **Swift River Reservation**. To the west, a scenic 2-mile loop links **Soapstone Hill** and the Gorge Trail in the Quabbin Reservoir lands, with many more miles of remote woods roads around. About 10 miles to the northeast, **Hubbardston State Forest** can be accessed from Mt. Jefferson; combine the Gates Hill, Old Cross, Over-the-Bridge, and Behind-the-Chimney Trails for a hilly, 4-mile figure-8 loop. **Town Farm Hill** in Barre also features a network of new, unmarked singletrack trails.

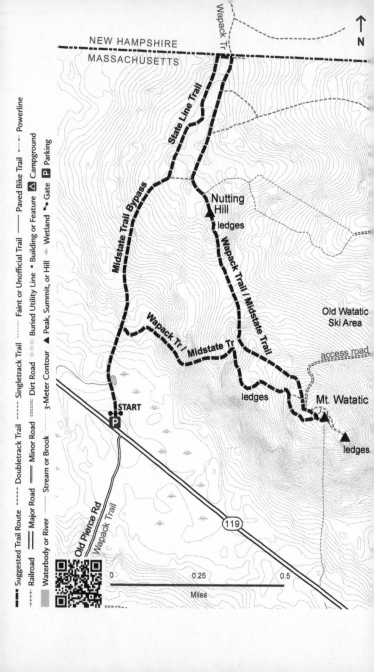

NEW HAMPSHIRE
MASSACHUSETTS

Wapack Tr

↑
N

State Line Trail

Midstate Trail Bypass

Nutting Hill
ledges

Wapack Trail / Midstate Trail

Old Watatic
Ski Area

access road

Wapack Tr / Midstate Tr

ledges

Mt. Watatic

ledges

START

P

Old Pierce Rd

Wapack Trail

119

- - Suggested Trail Route ---- Doubletrack Trail ----- Singletrack Trail ······ Faint or Unofficial Trail —— Powerline
++++ Railroad —— Major Road ====== Minor Road ···· Dirt Road ▦ Buried Utility Line ▪ Building or Feature △ Campground
—— Waterbody or River —— Stream or Brook ▦ Peak, Summit, or Hill ▲ Peak, Summit, or Hill ≋ Wetland ⌐ Gate P Parking

0   0.25   0.5

Miles

DISTANCE 3.5 Miles   **TOWN** Ashburnham
DIFFICULTY RATING Challenging   **TRAIL STYLE** Loop
TRAIL TYPE Singletrack/Doubletrack   **TOTAL ASCENT** 740 Feet

With its bald summit and rocky outcrops, Mt. Watatic beckons hikers and runners from far and wide. Trail types vary considerably, and the surface ranges from soft and gentle singletrack in some places to incredibly rocky and rooty steep slopes in others. For scenery, this site features spectacular views and pleasant woodland settings. The suggested loop is generally well marked and maintained by local trail stewards and DCR. Mt. Watatic is both the southern terminus of the long-distance Wapack Trail, which runs north into New Hampshire to its northern end at North Pack Monadnock Mountain, and the northern end of the Midstate Trail, which runs south to the Rhode Island state line. As such, this popular peak is often the staging site for all-day or even multiday adventures.

DIRECTIONS From Ashby, take Rte. 119 northwest for 5 miles to the small parking area for the Mt. Watatic trailhead on the right; look for the small brown Midstate Trail sign directly across the street. The parking lot often fills fast, so arrive early. There may also be limited parking along the northern shoulder of Rte. 119; obey any posted parking signs. **GPS** "Watatic Southern Terminus"

TRAIL From the trailhead, follow the main trail north down a slight slope into the woods. It quickly levels out and then crosses a wet area on bog bridges; this short portion is sometimes flooded in early spring. A wetland on the right makes a particularly nice breeding ground for thirsty mosquitoes (you've been warned!). Then begin climbing the slope at a gentle grade to a T-junction where the Wapack Trail / Midstate Trail goes right.

Stay straight and continue climbing the slope at a moderate grade on the wide Midstate Trail Bypass, following blue blazes and markers. This section is an old cart path, and the footing is particularly rocky and rooty here. After slowly curving to the right, arrive at a junction about a half mile up from the previous one.

Go left/north on the Midstate Trail Bypass / State Line Trail. The soft, gently undulating trail is quite runnable here, passing through stone walls and fern patches, and some poison ivy as well. In 0.4 miles you'll arrive at the Massachusetts–New Hampshire state line where there is a stone survey monument at a stone wall. Go right, keeping the stone wall to your left, and soon arrive at the Wapack Trail.

Optional Extension Going 1.25 miles north on the Wapack Trail into New Hampshire brings you to the quiet western shore of Binney Pond. Most of this section consists of gently rolling doubletrack; follow the yellow triangles (there are several unmarked junctions along the way). The top of Pratt Mountain, another mile farther north, features a terrific scenic vista overlooking the pond.

Go right and begin heading south up the wide Wapack Trail / Midstate Trail, which is marked with yellow triangle blazes and initially parallels a stone wall on the left. The grade is gentle for this stretch, and the surface is soft dirt with occasional stones. Several unmarked paths descend the slope to the east, linking up with the overgrown ski trails of the former Mt. Watatic Ski Area in what is now Ashby Wildlife Management Area.

At a Y-junction where a short trail leads right back to the Midstate Trail Bypass, bear slightly left and stay on the Wapack Trail. You'll cross into Mt. Watatic Reservation and soon emerge out onto open ledges on Nutting Hill. The actual top is marked with a large stone cairn. From there, zigzag down the rocky trail, narrower now, to a wooded saddle.

Rise at a moderate grade over rocks and roots below a dark conifer canopy. After passing a dirt road, arrive at the open summit of

1,832-foot Mt. Watatic where there are 360-degree views; you can often see Boston in the distance. A small warren of paths surrounds the top. The eastern summit, which boasts a similar open view, is accessible via a short spur trail leading southeast.

From the top, the Wapack Trail / Midstate Trail enters the woods just to the west at a sign. The grade is gradual at first as you pass several unmarked paths on the right. After passing a semi-open ledge about 0.25 miles from the top, swing left and drop steeply down through a dark hemlock forest. The trail is very rocky and rooty here, and you'll need to pay careful attention to your footing (as well as the trail markings). Near the bottom, pass through a split boulder and arrive back at the junction with the Midstate Trail Bypass. Go left and return back to the trailhead.

Alternate Route An alternate way up and down Watatic is to use the steep trail on the south side that follows the path of an old power line. This unofficial trail, essentially a rock scramble, starts from an unmarked trailhead about 0.75 miles east of the main one and climbs a half mile straight up the slope to the main summit.

NEARBY Heading north from Watatic, the 21-mile **Wapack Trail** crosses several rocky summits and makes a challenging but fun and scenic trail run. It's one of New England's oldest trails, built in the 1920s and named for the "Wa" in *Watatic* and the "Pack" in *Pack Monadnock*. Just across Rte. 119, the **Midstate Trail** follows Old Pierce Road south for a half mile to Steel Road, crosses it, becomes a singletrack path for 1.8 miles and passes over 1,536-foot Fisher Hill, and then reaches Rte. 101 north of Ashburnham. From there it can be followed all the way to Leominster State Forest and beyond on its 91-mile route to Rhode Island. About 12 miles southwest, a mostly flat, easy-to-moderate 2-mile blue-blazed trail loops around **Perley Brook Reservoir** in Gardner; look for the small red parking sign on Beagle Club Road. Other trails continue north into Gardner Forest.

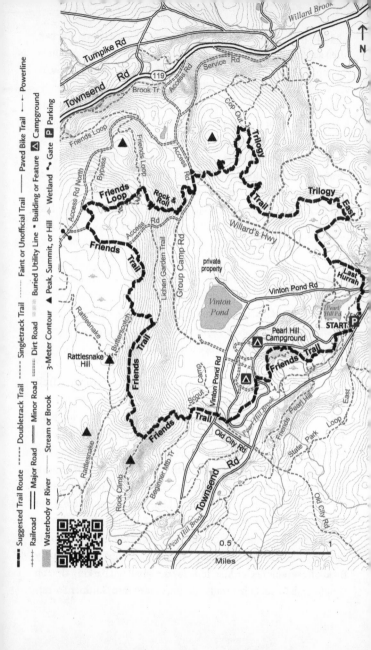

DISTANCE 6.6 Miles **TOWNS** Ashby and Townsend
DIFFICULTY RATING Moderate/Challenging **TRAIL STYLE** Loop
TRAIL TYPE Singletrack **TOTAL ASCENT** 690 Feet

Rocks, hills, brooks, trees, and mountain laurel—that's primarily what you'll encounter at Willard Brook State Forest and Pearl Hill State Park, though there are also ponds, wetlands, and old abandoned buildings, too (Pearl Hill is the part around the pond, campground, and parking lot; Willard Brook is the rest of the site). This suggested route combines various trail types for a fun run that samples much of what the site has to offer. Note that several trails here share similar names (three include the word Friends) and should not be confused for each other. The first half of this run is easy to moderate and quite easy to follow, despite many junctions and intersections (just look for yellow blazes); the second half is considerably more challenging, in terms of both terrain and navigation. Each part is rewarding for different reasons.

DIRECTIONS From Rte. 2, exit 100, take Rte. 13 north from Leominster for 6 miles. Turn left onto West Townsend/Lunenburg Road and go 3.5 miles north. Turn left onto Wyman Road. In 0.2 miles, turn left again onto New Fitchburg Road and go 0.6 miles to the large paved parking lot on the right.
GPS "Pearl Hill State Park, 105 New Fitchburg Road"

TRAIL Starting at the parking area, follow the campground road west into the park. After crossing over Pearl Hill Brook, a sign on the left marks the Friends Trail trailhead. Enter the woods and follow the yellow-blazed trail (also blazed orange for the first quarter mile). Stay on the well-marked Friends Trail; there are many junctions and intersections, and it crosses over the paved campground road twice. The footing is smooth as you roll along the constantly undulating terrain. Several side trails lead left to views across a wetland and can be combined for a short loop around the basin.

At about 1 mile, the Friends Trail reaches Vinton Pond Road. Cross it and follow the trail out into the open field; the blazes start up again on the far side. Bear left at a Y-junction and then right at another, then climb steadily up the east slope of Rattlesnake Hill. The footing is rough as you rise over occasional ledges. From a Y-junction, Friends Trail bears right and descends the slope at a gentle grade to a fork by a marked rock. Turn sharply left and begin climbing again to a junction with Butterscotch Trail.

Bear right and follow Friends Trail north to a dirt road. This section is somewhat rocky, with a few sharp turns at a stone wall. Go left on the dirt road and cross over the height of land just east of Fort Hill. At an unmarked junction, turn right and follow the red-blazed trail, curving left at a gentle grade. Note that this is now Friends Loop Trail, not Friends Trail.

At a junction with a dirt road, stay right on the red-blazed Friends Loop Trail and follow it east. Stay right at a junction with the Bypass Trail. In 0.2 miles, bear left at a junction. A slightly longer alternate route to the right of the main trail is well worth taking, as it winds very sharply back and forth across a series of rocky ledges. Soon after the alternate route rejoins the main path, go right on an unblazed trail (Rock & Roll) where the Friends Loop Trail bears left.

Optional Extension The red-blazed Friends Loop Trail is a 2-mile circuit through the northwest part of the forest. It passes near Damon Pond, which has a swimming area and restroom facilities, and can be combined with parts of the Brook Trail for a pleasant 2- to 3-mile extension of the suggested route.

Descend the slope for about a half mile. The footing in this section is generally smooth, but nevertheless it's rather technical as you begin a fun, roller-coastery descent over a series of ledges with sharp turns and steep drops. The trail ends at a junction with a dirt road. Go left/ north on the dirt road. Take a sharp right at the sign with an arrow pointing to Pearl Hill, and go southeast on Willard's Highway, a doubletrack trail. You'll immediately arrive at a junction.

Turn left and begin climbing on Trilogy Trail, a narrow, winding path that will be a highlight of this route for experienced trail runners. After an initial rise, the trail rolls up and down the hillside, rapidly twisting and turning back and forth as it goes. Stay right on Trilogy Trail at a junction with a faint trail called Cop Out, then cross over several forested ledges and small rocky hills. This section is quite technical in places. Eventually, it levels out and crosses a dirt road.

Stay straight on Trilogy East, and follow it for a half mile over low hills to a junction with a dirt road; though hilly, this section is as smooth, rock free, and pleasant as it gets. A fun extension of Trilogy unofficially continues on the other side of the road, but turn right and go 0.3 miles south to Willard's Highway. Turn left, and then almost immediately go left at a junction with Last Hurrah Trail. This singletrack path quickly climbs to and then traverses the crest of a narrow esker above a stream. It then drops steeply and ends at Vinton Pond Road. Turn left and cross over Pearl Hill Brook. Just past the bridge, go right to return to the trailhead, which is just past the trees at the far end of the open field.

NEARBY In northwest Fitchburg, runners will find many miles of gentle trails at the hills of the **Crocker Conservation Area**, accessible from Burbank Hospital or the upper end of Flat Rock Road. Overlook, Roey's Ramble, Big's Switchback, and Lower Loop Trails are all fun to run. Several miles to the northeast, across the Squannacook River, a number of relatively easy mixed singletrack/doubletrack loops can be made from the large Dudley Road parking area at **Townsend State Forest**.

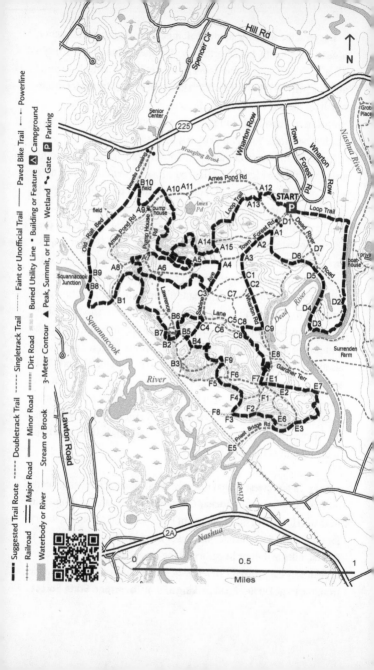

DISTANCE 9 Miles   **TOWN** Groton
DIFFICULTY RATING Easy/Moderate   **TRAIL STYLE** Loop
TRAIL TYPE Singletrack/Doubletrack   **TOTAL ASCENT** 480 Feet

Groton Town Forest features a dense network of rolling woodland trails that visit quiet streamsides, marshes, and kettle ponds. Most of it is relatively flat, though there are frequent small hills throughout. There are 14 miles of trails in total, with three marked loop options: the 9-mile and 3.4-mile trail race loops (marked in one direction only, with silver and blue arrows, respectively) and the 6.4-mile Town Forest Loop (marked in both directions with green arrows). This route roughly follows the silver arrows of the long-course loop, combining a number of different trail types in a wide-ranging tour. The description heavily references the junction numbers marked on small signs at major intersections. With such a complex system of trails and only minor topographic variation throughout, it's an especially easy site to get turned around in. Just keep following the silver arrows.

DIRECTIONS   From Rte. 119 in Groton, take Pleasant Street 0.3 miles west to Rte. 111. Go left and follow Rte. 111 south for 0.2 miles. Turn right on Rte. 225, and go 1.2 miles west. Turn left on Town Forest Road, and proceed south past the Wharton Row loop road to the small dirt parking area at the end.
GPS   "Town Forest Road, Groton"

TRAIL   From the trailhead at D1, head west on the Loop Trail. It's marked with silver arrows in white circles and green arrows in white circles; pay attention to the silver ones. Follow the markers along soft singletrack trail to Ames Pond Road (A12). Go left on this dirt road for a few hundred feet, then take a right back onto singletrack at A13.

For the next 2 miles, the trail winds around a series of small kettlehole ponds, rising and falling sharply on short, sometimes steep pitches. This is a fairly convoluted section of the route; there are many junctions, and you'll nearly double back on yourself several times. The first kettle pond comes into view through the woods on the left. Then you'll see one on the right and soon after pass between the two. While climbing a hill on the other side of the low area, pass a junction (A14) on the left, and then turn sharply right at A15 onto a trail that ambles through the woods above a pond. Follow this hilly stretch for about a quarter of a mile. At A5, go left on Town Forest Road for 0.25 miles. At A4, go right on Sabine Avenue.

At a near-5-way junction (C3), go right and follow the winding singletrack path straight across Lawrence Lane near A6, then across two more wide paths. The trail climbs lots of steep little hills in this section, but it has great flow and is enjoyably swoopy with few junctions. In about a mile you'll cross Ames Pond Road at A10, then reach Pump House Road at A9. Follow the road around to the right through an open field, and then turn sharply left at B10.

Go southwest on the dirt rail trail for 0.5 miles to Squannacook Junction (B9). Cross over the track remains and the straight path that parallels their east side. You'll briefly see the Squannacook River off to the right. Go straight at B8 where a side trail leads to the riverbank, recross the tracks, and bear right at a "Groton Town Forest" sign (B1). Follow this gentle singletrack trail for 0.5 miles to B7. Bear right, then go left at B2 at the bottom of the hill, where several trails branch to the right (but don't turn *hard* left into the shed).

Climb the steep hill, and then cross straight over Lawrence Lane. The trail switches tightly back and forth for about a quarter of a mile. At a fork, bear right up a short hill on a slightly wider path. At C4 (Sabine Avenue), turn right onto wide doubletrack. Turn left at B5, then left again at B4. Go straight through F9, then descend and go straight through F5. Descend a curvy trench section, and then bear right at F4. Curve hard left at F3, bear right at F2, turn right at E6, and finally turn sharply left at the bottom of the hill just above the river.

Stay straight at Priest Bridge Road (E3), and wind your way east and then north to E7. Go left and follow the wide path up the hill. Go straight at E1, then turn right onto narrow singletrack at F7. The next half mile or so winds back and forth through mostly flat pine forest with soft footing. Stay straight/right at the first C8, then turn right at the second C8. Go left at Warton Road (C9), and follow the wide, straight woods road north for almost a half mile.

> *Optional Trim/Alternate Route* For a nice singletrack alternative to the next half mile, go several hundred feet north on Wharton Road, then bear sharp right onto singletrack at an unmarked junction. This trail winds along the terrace above Dead River, then drops down to a low area with a rickety bridge before rejoining the suggested route, where you bear right.

Stay straight at C2 and C1 where trails lead left/west, then bear right at A3 onto Town Forest Road. Stay straight at A2, then go hard right at A1. Descend at a moderate grade, passing an unmarked trail on the right along the way, to the banks of Dead River (an old channel of the Nashua River). Winding gently along the edge of this oxbow pond, stay right at D6, D5, and D4. At D3, a side trail leads right out to a view across the Nashua River. The trail then swings left. Go north along the west bank of the river. Watch for poison ivy lining the sides of the trail here. Pass several junctions (including D2) with trails leading left. At a sharp turn, swing left and head slightly uphill over tree roots, with a residential neighborhood off to the right, to the trailhead.

NEARBY A network of wide trails at **Lawrence Woods**, **Sabine Woods**, and **Surrenden Farms** can be accessed from **Groton Place** on the east side of the Nashua River. To the northeast, Groton's **Gamlin**

Crystal Spring Conservation Area consists of two networks of well-maintained trails for nonmotorized use, with the smaller western one featuring some cool geology and the eastern one including paths along a tall streamside esker. **Wharton Plantation** and **McClain's Woods** in Groton and **Peabody** and **Lane Conservation Areas**, "Large" Town Forest, and **Cowdrey Nature Center** in Lunenburg all offer sizable and highly runnable trail systems. The flat and scenic **Oxbow Loop** and **Eagle Loop** trails flank the banks of the Nashua River at **J. Harry Rich State Forest** in Groton. Lightly marked trails at the old quarries on **Flatrock Hill** in Dunstable can be somewhat rough and rugged but have interesting potential and connect multiple conservation areas.

DISTANCE 11 Miles   **TOWNS** Princeton, Leominster, and Westminster
DIFFICULTY RATING Moderate/Challenging   **TRAIL STYLE** Loop
TRAIL TYPE Singletrack/Dirt Road   **TOTAL ASCENT** 1,130 Feet

Leominster State Forest encompasses a number of interesting natural landscape features, including big hills, small hills, forested ledges, open ledges, cliffs, and ponds. It is laced with a network of dirt roads and trails of all types and abuts several other properties with trail systems. This loop samples a variety of the forest's features in the central section and can easily be shortened or extended at many points. The first part, over Wolf Den Hill east of Paradise Pond, is challenging to navigate; the more remote parts are also notably difficult to follow after leaves have fallen. The second part, over Ball Hill, is better marked and easier to follow, though it also includes a greater amount of elevation change. There is a dense network of mountain bike singletrack on the lower east side of this property, easily accessible from the Elm Street parking lot, that is also worth exploring.

DIRECTIONS   From Rte. 2, exit 95, go 3 miles south on Rte. 31 (Princeton/Fitchburg Road) to the turn for the dirt Rocky Pond Lot parking area on the left/east side of the road; look for a small brown "Rocky Pond Road" sign on a tree. Alternate parking can be found slightly farther north either at the Crow Hill climbing area lot (Ledges Lot; west side of Princeton Road) or at Crow Hills Pond (Princeton Lot; east side of road).

GPS   "71 Rocky Pond Road, Princeton"

TRAIL   From the parking lot, follow Rocky Pond Road east from the gate. In 0.1 miles, bear right onto an unmarked singletrack trail. Go

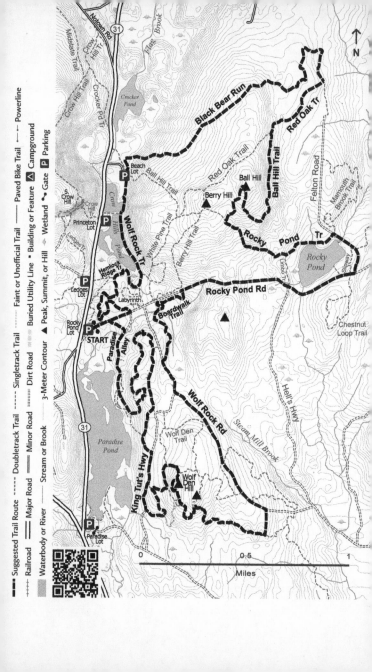

0.1 miles, and then turn right onto Paradise Alley. Descend gradually for 0.4 miles, passing unmarked junctions with smaller trails on the left and right. At a braid in the road, bear left. At a junction just past where the trail braids and starts climbing, turn left and climb at a steeper grade up a rocky slope. This trail soon levels off and curves left. The winding singletrack now undulates along the hillside, braiding a few times, and then swings right and climbs to an unmarked junction where a spur path leads left. Bear right and follow the trail along the crest of the hill. In 0.3 miles, bear right at another unmarked junction and keep descending. Stay left at the next junction and reach King Tut's Highway soon after.

Turn right and descend for 0.25 miles. Turn left onto singletrack at an unmarked junction and begin climbing. Bear left at the first junction and traverse the slope. In 0.2 miles, bear right at the next junction. Then climb briefly and turn left at a junction. Turn right at the next two junctions, and then pass over the top of 974-foot Wolf Den Hill. At a large boulder, bear left and drop down to a junction. Turn left and zigzag back and forth along the south side of the hill for 0.7 miles, crossing some forested ledges and stony low areas. At an unmarked junction, stay straight and keep descending. Then turn left at a junction and drop north down the slope to Wolf Rock Road.

Turn left on Wolf Rock Road and follow it for a mile or so back up toward Rocky Pond Road, passing several junctions with (fun) singletrack trail on the right along the way. After starting to descend and passing King Tut's Highway on the left, bear right on the blue-blazed Boardwalk Trail and follow it for 0.6 miles to Rocky Pond Road. Turn right and head due east for almost a mile, passing Limbo Trail leading left, Hell's Highway road on the right, an unmarked trail down toward Rocky Pond on the left, and Chestnut Loop Trail (a nice half-mile lollipop loop) on the right. Directly across from the Chestnut Loop on the left is another unmarked path (known as "Slipway") leading down toward Rocky Pond that can make a fine alternate singletrack route. Continue straight on Rocky Pond a few dozen more feet and then turn left on Fenton Road. Descending Fenton, pass an unmarked trail on the right and the lower end of Slipway on the left. Just past a short spur down to the pond, rise slightly to an intersection.

Turn left onto Rocky Pond Trail and follow it west. Stay straight at a junction with Limbo Trail on the left and climb at a moderate grade to a junction. Turn right and climb steeply on Ball Hill Trail to a 1,196-foot summit. From the top, descend south and then curve left to traverse the hillside for 0.5 miles to a junction. Turn right and descend at a gentle grade on Red Oak Trail to a junction with Fenton Road. Go left and descend gently north on Black Bear Run. The trail soon swings left, then climbs at varying grades for 0.6 miles, levels off and briefly traverses the north side of the hill, and then descends for 0.6 miles. At the bottom, bear left at an unmarked junction and climb to the paved Beach Lot parking area.

Go south, skirting the beach and tracing the east side of Lower Crow Hill Pond. At a junction, bear left and follow the mostly flat, yellow-blazed Wolf Rock Trail south along the shore of the upper pond. Bear right at a junction with an orange-blazed trail, then descend briefly, cross a boardwalk, and climb a short slope to a junction. Take the red-blazed Hemlock Ridge Trail right. Descend, cross a wet area, and then curve right and climb slightly along a stone-wall embankment to a peninsula where you can see the pond through the trees. Wind around to a junction. Stay straight/left on Hemlock Ridge Trail as it loops for 0.6 miles back to Rocky Pond Road. Go right to return to the parking lot.

Optional Extension(s) The Labyrinth: This extremely snaky half-mile loop trail nearly doubles back on itself multiple times before finishing where it starts. Crow Hill: West of Princeton Road is a network of challenging trails over and around Crow Hill. You can climb to the Midstate Trail from Beach Lot and then follow it south along the top of the ledges, or just create a loop from Rocky Pond Lot.

NEARBY To the east, you can link to a series of rocky but well-marked loop trails over **South** and **North Monoosnoc Mountains** (also accessible from trailheads below to the east and north); there's an expansive vista out over Leominster from a ledge on North Monoosnoc.

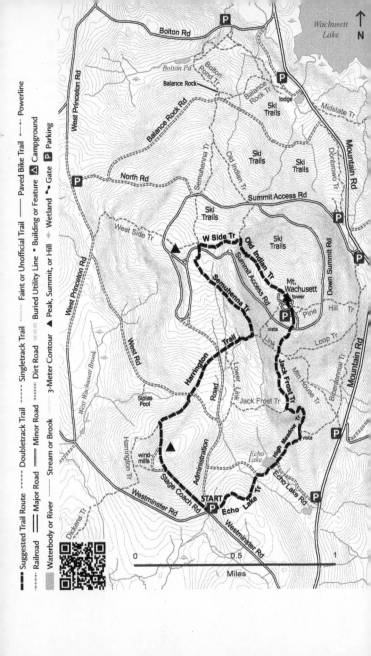

DISTANCE 4 Miles   **TOWNS** Westminster and Princeton
DIFFICULTY RATING Challenging   **TRAIL STYLE** Loop
TRAIL TYPE Singletrack   **TOTAL ASCENT** 770 Feet

Wachusett Mountain is one of the crown-jewel peaks of central Massachusetts. At 2,006 feet, it is the state's highest point east of the Connecticut River and offers excellent 360-degree views. Trails, including the Midstate Trail that leads to other sites like Crow Hills, Leominster State Forest, and Wachusett Meadows, cover all of the slopes and can be linked together for long, challenging runs. The terrain is generally steep and rocky (sometimes very much so), though softer and gentler trails can be found on some of the lower slopes, particularly on the mountain's south and west sides.

DIRECTIONS   From Rte. 2, exit 92, go 2 miles south on Rte. 140. Turn right on Park Road and go 3.7 miles south. Take a very sharp right on Westminster Road and go 0.8 miles. The hiking trailhead is on the right; there is a very small parking area in front of a wooden Echo Lake Trail sign and some roadside parking slightly farther along on the right on Westminster Road (do not block the gates of the access roads). If this parking area is full, use the large lot at the base of the ski area and try the Alternate Route below.
GPS   "Echo Lake Trail, 82 Westminster Road"

TRAIL   Starting at the Echo Lake Trail trailhead, follow the blue-blazed Echo Lake Trail up the rooty hillside. Go up and over the small hill to a junction with Echo Lake Road just past a bridge over East Wachusett Brook. Turn right and follow the dirt road, descending to the pond on the left. At the far side of the pond, go straight at a junction by an old fireplace on High Meadow Trail. Climb steadily up the rocky slope to the meadow.

At a junction with Bicentennial Trail at the upper end of the meadow, continue straight on High Meadow trail and climb steeply around rock ledges to a junction. Turn right onto Jack Frost Trail and follow it beneath a dark hemlock canopy along a relatively flat ridge. At an intersection, continue straight up the hill on Mountain House Trail, climbing steeply to the paved auto road. Cross the road and continue up a few hundred feet to a parking lot. Look for the yellow Midstate Trail markers and follow them, past a pond on the left, to the tower at the summit of Wachusett Mountain.

On the far side of the tower, look for the yellow markers of the Midstate Trail and the Old Indian Trail sign. Descend northwest on this trail to a junction, passing the upper end of a chairlift and several unmarked side trails along the way. Below some steep ledges, turn left onto West Side Trail and follow it across the slope to an intersection. Turn left and immediately cross the paved auto road.

On the other side of the road, take Semuhenna Trail southeast across the slope, descending slightly to an intersection. Turn right on Harrington Trail / Midstate Trail and follow the combined blue blazes and yellow triangle markers to a junction with Lower Link Trail. Stay straight and descend to a dirt road. Cross the road and descend to West Road. Cross West Road and go across the slope to a junction.

Turn left and climb on Stage Coach Trail, passing a clearing with some windmills on the right. At a junction with a dirt access road, bear left and descend at a steady grade for a quarter mile back to the trailhead.

Alternate Routes   Take the Midstate Trail from the ski area trailhead on the north side and follow it up past Balance Rock. From there, create a 3-mile loop using the Midstate, Semuhenna, Harrington, and Old Indian Trail paths. West Side Trail and Bolton Pond Trail are also excellent trails for running. Mountain House Trail can also be used, but it's very rough and rocky. Bicentennial Trail crosses the eastern slope of the mountain and is significantly more challenging than it looks, crossing several talus slopes and boulder fields. Several wide dirt roads are also excellent for running on softer surfaces and at gentler grades, including West Road, North Road, Echo Lake Road, and Balance Rock Road.

NEARBY Wachusett connects to **Leominster State Forest** (site 6) via a challenging but fun trail run over **Crow Hills** on the Midstate Trail. The Midstate Trail also leads south to the hills and wetlands of **Wachusett Meadows** (a Mass Audubon property) and beyond.

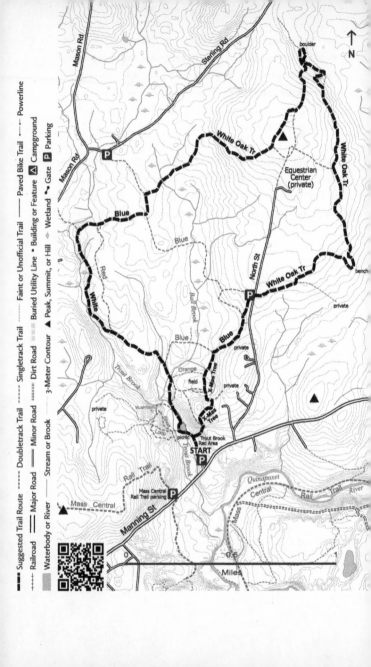

DISTANCE 6 Miles   **TOWN** Holden
DIFFICULTY RATING Moderate   **TRAIL STYLE** Loop
TRAIL TYPE Singletrack/Doubletrack   **TOTAL ASCENT** 430 Feet

Trout Brook Recreation Area and adjacent conservation land host a network of marked loop trails that are easily accessible from several entry points. The landscape is rolling hills, with a mix of trail surface types. Frequent rocky or rooty parts are mixed with fun, flowing smooth stretches. This loop offers a representative sampling of the terrain. It's mostly mature forest with no open vistas or standout features, though one trail follows the eponymous brook and several others cut through old fields or pass by wetlands. Old stone walls, cellar holes, wooden bridges, and glacial boulders are common throughout. The lower end near the picnic area is considerably more popular than the northern parts; by parking at the smaller lots you can usually avoid crowds entirely. Some portions can be muddy, soggy, or even flooded in the spring, especially on the Blue Trail.

DIRECTIONS   From Holden, take Rte. 31 north for 2 miles. Turn right onto Manning Street and go 0.9 miles to the spacious dirt parking lot on the left; look for the small green "Trout Brook Reservation" sign on a wooden post. Alternate parking can be found just to the west at the Central Mass Rail Trail (Jefferson) parking lot, at small lots to the north along Mason Road and Sterling Road, and at a small lot for the White Oak Conservation Area along North Street.

GPS   "Trout Brook Recreation Area, Holden"

TRAIL   From the main parking area, follow the dirt road through the gate with the big TROUT BROOK letters on it north to a junction by a small pond. Keeping the picnic pavilion to your left and the pond on your right, cross a bridge and trace the left/west side of the pond. Curve right and then left to enter the woods north of the pond. Follow the flat, wide, rooty trail north through dark woods to a junction with two bridges (where the Short Trail loop leads left over Trout Brook to the Mushroom Trail).

Bear right at the junction and begin climbing a rooty trail blazed with red, white, and blue triangle markers. Stay left at a junction where Green Trail leads up to the right. Stay left at two more junctions, still following red/white/blue triangle markers. At the next junction, stay left on the red/white trail while Blue Trail veers right. At the next junction, stay left on White Trail while Red Trail bears right (Red Trail makes a perfectly good and in some ways gentler alternative to White Trail here). White Trail then rolls along the east bank of Trout Brook for 0.6 miles, with several short, unmarked spurs leading left. Turn right at a junction just past some boardwalks and go 0.1 miles to a junction with a "Red Trail" sign.

Go left on Blue Trail (a.k.a. Bob Elms Trail), passing a narrow unmarked cutoff link to Red Trail on the right. Follow Blue Trail across a wet area to a junction. Turn left on the yellow-blazed White Oak Trail. Take a sharp right at a junction and follow White Oak Trail for 0.8 miles across a wet area and up a hill. At two junctions near the top, stay left on White Oak Trail. Descend at a gentle grade for 0.3 miles to a junction near a large, lichen-covered boulder (called "Dinosaur Rocks").

Curving sharply right after the boulder, follow the yellow blazes south as the trail rises and falls slightly along the east side of the hill. After cutting through a dark, thick stand of mountain laurel and passing a spring, the forest opens back up again beneath oak and pine. At 0.6 miles past the hairpin turn, stay straight at a junction near a propped-up granite obelisk called Two Town Stone. From there, continue 0.5 miles south to a bench near the remains of a big oak tree.

Then curve right and climb to a wet area with several braided strands of trail (all just alternate branches that reconnect). At 0.6 miles from the bench, cross North Street.

Bearing left, follow a short, unnamed trail down to Blue Trail. Go left on Blue Trail. Stay right where several trails lead left off-property, then descend to a junction. Go left on the green-marked X-Mas Tree Trail, staying right at unmarked junctions. Pass an orange-blazed path on the right and climb through an overgrown meadow. Stay straight at two unmarked junctions with trails leading right. Back in the woods, stay right on X-Mas Tree Trail at a junction. Cross the top of a hill, and then begin descending. Cross over an unmarked trail, and then drop steeply down to the entrance road. Go left to return to the parking area.

Ferns along the X-Mas Tree Trail at Trout Brook in Holden.

Optional Extensions   Several other loop options are possible, using the color-blazed trails mentioned above as well as the Mushroom Trail and (surprisingly hilly) Short Trail west of the brook.

NEARBY   From several nearby parking areas, you can access the **Mass Central Rail Trail (MCRT)**, which runs along the banks of the Quinapoxet River between Holden and West Boylston. Numerous unmarked footpaths branch off this wide trail. Sections of the MCRT in Rutland/Barre are also good for running. Several miles to the east, there's a network of dirt forest roads between Rte. 110 and the north shore of **Wachusett Reservoir**, accessible from a number of gates. **Green Hill Park** in Worcester provides a short trail-running experience that's simultaneously rugged and urban, and it includes the **East Side Trail**, a section of the city's 14-mile **East-West Trail / Four-Town Greenway**.

DISTANCE 5.6 Miles   **TOWNS** Berlin and Northborough
DIFFICULTY RATING Moderate   **TRAIL STYLE** Loop
TRAIL TYPE Singletrack/Doubletrack   **TOTAL ASCENT** 720 Feet

This Mt. Pisgah (there's four in the state) sits near the southern end of Shrewsbury Ridge and features several expansive views of the surrounding landscape. An extensive system of well-marked and -blazed trails can be accessed from three separate trailheads. The trails wind through the forest and lead to several scenic vistas, gorges, vernal pools, glacial erratics, and more. The dense network of technical loops at the southern end is especially enjoyable for running. There are some unmaintained trails at the northern and southern ends that aren't shown on maps.

DIRECTIONS From Berlin (easily accessible from both I-495 and I-290), go 0.7 miles west on Linden Street to (unsigned) roadside parking on the left/south. Alternate parking can be found along Smith Road in Northborough and along Lyman Road on the Berlin/Northborough town line.

GPS "MTB Mt. Pisgah, 120 Linden Street, Berlin"

TRAIL From the roadside pull-off, take the red-blazed Berlin Road doubletrack trail up the hill to the right. In a half mile, after crossing over and descending the hill, go right at a junction to stay on Berlin Road. Climb for about a half mile to a junction just past a boardwalk, passing junctions on the right and then left and briefly sharing blazes with green and then yellow. Keep climbing on Berlin Road, steeply at first. Where it starts to level off, bear left onto an unmarked side trail; this quarter-mile singletrack path runs along the upper edge

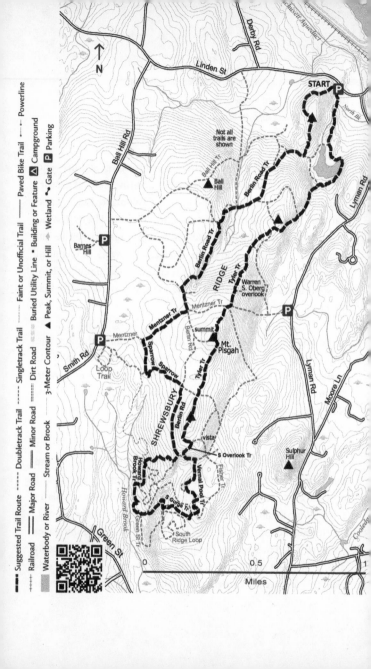

Legend

▮ Suggested Trail Route	---- Doubletrack Trail
---- Singletrack Trail	---- Faint or Unofficial Trail
══ Railroad	══ Major Road
══ Minor Road	═══ Dirt Road
~~ Waterbody or River	─── Stream or Brook
── Paved Bike Trail	·+·+· Powerline
═══ Buried Utility Line	▪ Building or Feature
▲ Campground	▲ Peak, Summit, or Hill
⟿ Wetland	⤫ Gate
P Parking	

START P

North Bk

Derby Rd

Linden St

Ball Hill Rd

▲ Ball Hill

Barnes Hill P

RIDGE

Berlin Road Tr

Tyler Tr

Warren S. Oberg overlook

Lyman Rd

Mentzner Tr

Mentzner Tr

summit

Berlin Rd

Mt. Pisgah

P

Smith Rd

P

Loop Trail

Sparrow

Sparrow Tr

Tyler Tr

SHREWSBURY

Berlin Rd

Moore Ln

Sulphur Hill ▲

Lyman Rd

vista

S Overlook Tr

Howard Brook Tr

Green St Tr

Vernal Pool Tr

Fisher Tr

S Gorge Tr

South Ridge Loop

Howard Brook

Green St

Cooledge

Not all trails are shown

0   0.5   1
Miles

of a scenic forested ravine (be careful on the steep ledges) and along a stone wall to a junction at the top. Above the ravine, turn left and go to an intersection.

Turn right on blue-blazed Mentzner Trail and descend gradually to a junction (right leads down to Smith Road trailhead). Turn left onto white-blazed Sparrow Trail. In 0.15 miles, bear left at a junction and gently climb 0.2 miles up switchbacks on Sparrow Trail. At an intersection with red-blazed Berlin Road, take a right and go south for 0.3 miles. This is where it starts to get a bit convoluted. Turn right at a junction with Howard Brook Trail and then immediately turn right again at another junction. Descend 0.2 miles to a junction with Howard Brook Trail and turn left. Go right at three successive junctions, and then a left (where Green Street Trail goes right), to stay on Howard Brook Trail. Then turn right on South Gorge Trail and climb to a junction.

Optional Extension   To add a very fun extra half mile, continue straight onto the South Ridge Loop trail. This lollipop loop winds around a bench on the hillside, gently rising and falling as it swoops back and forth.

Go left on South Gorge Trail and climb east to a junction with Vernal Pool Trail. Go right and then immediately left to stay on Vernal Pool. Go north for 0.4 miles to a junction. Go left up Berlin Road to a junction, then right up South Overlook Trail to a junction. Make a quick out-and-back to the South View scenic vista, then return to the junction and climb the yellow-blazed Tyler Trail north for a half mile to the summit (crossing over Sparrow Trail along the way). There is no view at the top, but it's marked with U.S. Geological Survey markers and a cairn.

From the top, continue north on Tyler Trail for 0.25 miles to a scenic view at Warren S. Oberg Overlook ledge, crossing over Mentzner Trail along the way. Continue north on Tyler Trail and descend 0.3 miles to a junction, passing two trails descending to the right. Where Tyler Trail goes left, bear right on the blue-blazed trail that descends down off the ridge, somewhat steeply in places, to a junction just above a pond. Go right and head north around the east side of the pond to a junction. Stay straight and cross over a few low rolling hills to return to the trailhead.

NEARBY Seven miles southeast, a network of trails and old roads links **Westboro Wildlife Management Area**, **Cedar Hill**, **Crane Swamp**, **Sawink Farm**, and **Walnut Hill**; best access is from the **Lake Chauncy** trailhead parking in Westborough. About 7 miles northeast in Bolton, **Rattlesnake Hill** is the town's largest conservation area and supports a dense network of rugged, hilly, mostly singletrack trails. Start at the Bob Horton Loop Trail and Lime Kiln site on the east end, then continue west to the winding Ridge Loop and Split Rock trails; access from a small parking area along Rte. 85. Bolton's **Vaughn Hills** and **Bowers Springs** conservation lands together feature nearly ten miles of hilly but very scenic and runnable trails.

DISTANCE 5.2 Miles   **TOWN** Sturbridge

DIFFICULTY RATING Easy/Moderate/Challenging   **TRAIL STYLE** Loop

TRAIL TYPE Singletrack/Doubletrack/Dirt Road   **TOTAL ASCENT** 440 Feet

Just southwest of Old Sturbridge village, a dense network of trails centered at Leadmine Mountain Conservation Area offers loops of nearly any difficulty level. The markings and signs of all the major trails are color coded. There are some completely flat sections around ponds that are great for anyone new to trail running and a number of intermediate and significantly more challenging trails, including a fairly technical one appropriately called the Knife Edge. A scenic highlight of the site is the amazing blue color of one of the ponds when water levels are high enough; it almost looks like a glacial lake out west. Though an east-side parking area is used for the suggested route, the site can be accessed from a parking area on the west side as well.

DIRECTIONS From I-84, exit 5, go west on Old Sturbridge Village Road for 0.1 miles to the entrance for the spacious main parking area on the left. There is a much smaller parking lot with space for several vehicles about a half mile south along Old Sturbridge Village Road/Shattuck Road.

GPS "Leadmine Mountain Trail (Main Entrance)"

TRAIL Heading south from the parking area, pass a gate and follow the wide dirt lane of Morgan Track Trail. Stay straight where a trail leads to the right. At 0.3 miles, turn right onto the wide, purple-blazed Camp Robinson Crusoe Trail.

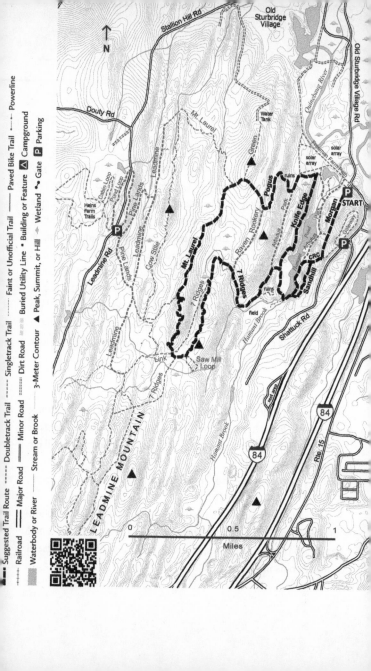

Optional Extension   To add a fun extra mile to your run, turn left and follow Camp Robinson Crusoe Trail up the hill. Just before the parking lot at the top, bear left and follow the purple-and-black-blazed Gateway Trail loop back around to the same spot. This is an especially enjoyable and fairly easy little loop. Then drop back down Camp Robinson Crusoe to the junction.

In 0.1 miles, turn left off of Camp Robinson Crusoe and begin climbing Sand Hill Trail. This path crosses over a small hill and then drops down to Arbutus Park Trail. Turn left and follow the blue-blazed Arbutus Park Trail around the south end of the pond, where an unmarked trail leads left. Stay left at a junction with Knife Edge Trail. Curving left, pass a junction where Arbutus Park Trail goes right and follow the yellow-blazed Seven Ridges Trail up the hill. Stay straight where a path leads left up a hill. Then curve right and climb to a junction where Raven Rookery Trail leads right. Bear left and keep following Seven Ridges Trail up the hill. It skirts a wet area and then bears left to head south. At 0.25 miles from Raven Rookery Trail, turn left at a junction with an unmarked singletrack trail on the left. Follow this rugged trail along the ledges of a forested ridge for half a mile to an intersection.

Bear right on the yellow-blazed Saw Mill Trail and quickly arrive at a junction where the Seven Ridges Trail leads left (this trail makes a good optional extension, adding another mile or more to your route). Stay right at the junction and drop down to a 4-way intersection where The Link trail leads left and Seven Ridges leads right. Stay straight and follow the unmarked trail up the hill. This fun singletrack path winds back and forth north for 0.6 miles to a junction with Mt. Laurel Trail.

Optional Extension(s)   To reach the excellent Heins Farm trail network, take Mt. Laurel Trail left to Leadmine Trail. Bear right onto Leadmine and then go left on Pinelands Trail and follow it up to the Heins Farm parking area. It's about a mile from the start of this extension up to that trailhead. From there, several short loops are possible on Pond Loop (0.7 miles; wide and accessible), Cabin Loop (0.5 miles; past a wetland), and Stafford Loop (1.2 miles; very scenic through fields). On the return trip, Cow Stile Trail makes a fun half-mile addition as it scoots along the crest of a wooded ridge.

Turn right and follow the green-and-white-blazed Mt. Laurel Trail. This wide path undulates though the forest to a junction with the upper end of Raven Rookery Trail. Turn right on the green-blazed Raven Rookery and descend to a junction with the blue-green-blazed Pogus Village Trail. Turn left and descend, passing some old buildings left of the trail, to a junction with Arbutus Park Trail. Turn left and follow the blue-blazed Arbutus Park Trail north. It soon curves right and descends to a junction.

Turn right and take the Knife Edge Trail. This fun, challenging singletrack path straddles the spine of a low, forested ridge above the pond down to the left. In just over a half mile, it brings you back to the blue-blazed Arbutus Park Trail. From here, turn left and follow the trail back to the parking lot.

NEARBY A few miles north, a fun short run can be made at **Opacum Woods**, accessible from a trailhead at the end of Old Brook Cir; combine the White/Green, Blue, Yellow, and Red Trails (and a rough out-and-back spur to Perry's Point on Opacum Pond) for a scenic, moderately challenging 3-mile loop. East of I-84, **Westville Lake Recreation Area** in Southbridge offers several miles of easy running on wide, groomed paths, while wilder, unmarked trails at **Breakneck Brook WMA** in Sturbridge are worth exploring. A section of the **Grand Trunk Rail Trail** about 6 miles to the west, off Rte. 20 in Brimfield, provides an excellent introduction to trail running with its blend of wide dirt rail trail and flat, easy singletrack paths.

DISTANCE 6.5 Miles **TOWN** Sturbridge
DIFFICULTY RATING Moderate **TRAIL STYLE** Loop
TRAIL TYPE Singletrack/Doubletrack **TOTAL ASCENT** 630 Feet

More than 10 miles of trails wind through Wells State Park. The rugged landscape is dominated by several forested north–south ridges interspersed with ponds and wetlands in between, though there's a substantial amount of gentler terrain, too. There is a day-use fee, and it also has a camping area, cabins, picnic areas, and a swimming beach for campers. The trails, most of which are a mix of singletrack and doubletrack, are generally well blazed and maintained, though most are not actually marked with trail signs. This route loops around a large part of the park and includes several worthwhile scenic vistas. Most of it is in the woods and away from crowds, though the final part is on paved park roads through the busy campground. Overall, the park feels quite remote despite its proximity to the Mass Pike, and it's easy to find a significant amount of peace and solitude.

DIRECTIONS From Sturbridge (near the junction of the Mass Pike and I-84), take Rte. 20 east for about 2 miles. Turn left on Rte. 41 and go 1 mile north. Turn left onto Wells State Park Road and go 1.2 miles west to the large paved parking lot on the right.
GPS "Wells State Park; 159 Walker Pond Road"

TRAIL Starting at the main parking area, follow the paved park road east for 0.1 miles to the trailhead at a gate on the left. Follow the green-blazed Walker Pond Trail, an old gravel road, due north. Along the way you'll pass under some power lines and parallel a wetland off to the left. The footing is a little rough in places, but otherwise it's flat and easy.

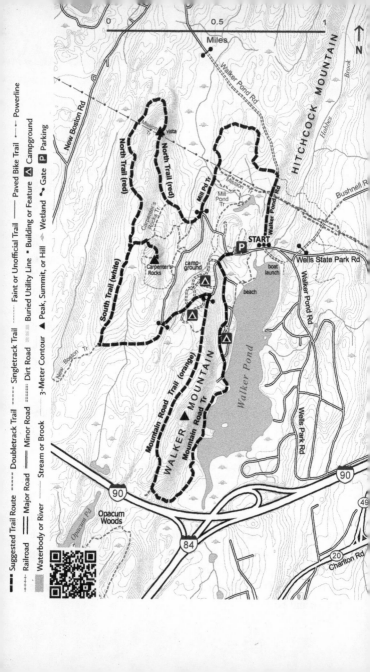

At a big rock with a large green rectangle painted on it, bear left. Follow the narrow green-blazed trail over flattish yet still lightly rolling and highly runnable terrain. There's a fair bit of poison ivy lining the trail in this lower section. Soon after crossing back under the power lines, you'll reach an unmarked junction with Mill Pond Trail (a wide, well-graded accessible path with occasional wooden bridges).

Go right on the accessible trail, still following green blazes. It rises at a gentle grade and eventually widens into a paved road. The trail veers off the paved road into the woods and parallels the road for a short distance. At a junction soon after, bear right. Now following green, red, and yellow blazes, go uphill. Two yellow-blazed trails branch off to the left; stay right on the red and green trail. Climb at an easy grade for a half mile to a scenic vista at the power lines where Mission Trail heads left. Stay straight. From there, descend somewhat steeply and then curve left, dropping down some ledges and starting to head south. Recross the power lines, crossing over Mission Trail, and then continue south on the red-blazed North Trail for 0.6 miles to a 3-way junction.

Take a left to make a short out-and-back (0.4 miles total) to a scenic vista up at Carpenter's Rocks. The trail descends a short way to a 3-way junction. Turn right here and then climb up to the vista at the top where there is a great view out over the valley to the east. Return back to the junction the way you came.

Optional Trim You can descend from Carpenter's Rocks on the yellow-blazed Carpenter's Rocks Trail, but the upper part is very rough and not great for running. There's also a narrow, unmarked path trail that descends from the top, first to the south and then east, but it's rough and not particularly fun to run beyond the first few hundred feet.

From the 3-way junction, descend at a gentle grade on South Trail to a junction with New Boston Trail. Go left/east on South Trail for

0.4 miles. The rugged doubletrack path gently falls and then rises along the slope here.

Veer right onto the paved park road and descend 0.25 miles, going the same direction as one-way traffic. Just past a green water tank on the right, take a sharp right onto the orange-blazed Walker Mountain Trail. Follow the wide old road along the right side of the ridge for nearly a mile to an unmarked junction near the south end. Here, a short spur leads down to an obstructed, fenced-off view of the highway. At the junction, go left and descend from the ridge, steeply at first and then more gently, curving to the left as you go, until the trail reaches the south end of Walker Pond. Follow the trail north along the shore of the pond until it ends at the campground road. Follow the road north through the campground toward the exit and trailhead parking.

NEARBY Several rolling trails can be combined for a short, scenic run at **Rock House Reservation** in West Brookfield. **Sibley Farm** in Spencer features trails through hilly woods and grassy fields (check for ticks). The trail system at **Moore State Park** in Paxton includes several short but well-signed scenic loops (such as Stairway Loop, Laurel Loop, Davis Hill Field, and Enchanta Trail), while **Spencer State Forest** offers a mix of unmarked doubletrack-width paths, rocky old roads, and short singletrack stretches.

DISTANCE 7 Miles   **TOWN** Charlton
DIFFICULTY RATING Moderate   **TRAIL STYLE** Loop
TRAIL TYPE Singletrack   **TOTAL ASCENT** 190 Feet

Buffumville Lake Trail rings a long, north-south flood-control impoundment at an Army Core of Engineers (ACOE) project area. The rolling path around the shoreline features an enjoyable mix of terrain types and difficulties, with smooth dirt sections, rocky spots, and muddy parts, along with quite a few semi-technical rooty stretches and small hills. Occasional signposts along the way assist with route finding and safety. Most of the loop is shaded, though there are open parts and many views of the lake. Several small tributary brook crossings lack bridges and are challenging to cross after heavy rainstorms. The main loop trail is well marked with blue paint blazes, though several other trails are also marked the same; when in doubt, choose the one closest to the lake. The loop can be halved by crossing the middle causeway on a narrow path beside the road; the southern loop is about 4.5 miles, and the northern loop is about 3 miles. Deerflies are often brutal in July, and a significant amount of poison ivy lines the trail. Dirt bikes are not allowed. There's also a swimmer's beach, picnic area, and disc-golf course.

DIRECTIONS   From I-395, exit 7B, go 3 miles west on Charlton Street/ Oxford Street to the large, signed parking area for Buffumville Park on the right. From Rte. 31 in Charlton, go southeast on Muggett Hill Road for 1.5 miles. Bear right onto Oxford Road and go 2.2 miles to the parking area on the left (just after crossing over the lake). Buffumville Park charges a small fee; there's also limited parking at the parking areas for the boat ramp and disc-golf course.
GPS   "Buffumville Lake Park"

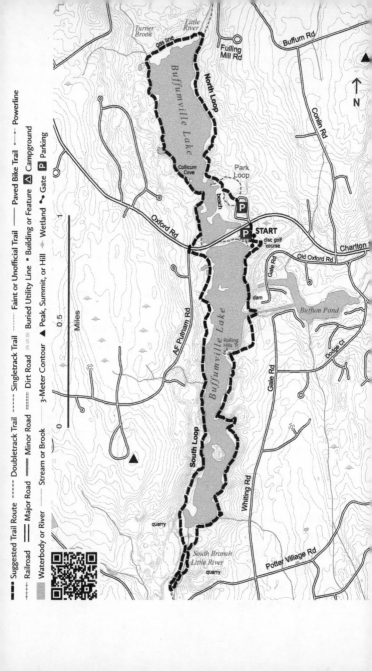

Legend:

- ■■ Suggested Trail Route
- ----- Doubletrack Trail
- ----- Singletrack Trail
- ····· Faint or Unofficial Trail
- --- Paved Bike Trail
- --+-- Powerline
- +++++ Railroad
- === Major Road
- ==== Minor Road
- ≡≡≡ Dirt Road
- ----- Buried Utility Line
- • Building or Feature
- ▲ Campground
- ---- Waterbody or River
- --- Stream or Brook
- ---- 3-Meter Contour
- ▲ Peak, Summit, or Hill
- ⟿ Wetland
- ⟡ Gate
- P Parking

Turner Brook

Little River

Buffum Rd

Fulling Mill Rd

gas line

Buffumville Lake

North Loop

Conlin Rd

N

Park Loop

Collicum Cove

beach

P

Oxford Rd

P START

disc golf course

Charlton

Old Oxford Rd

Gale Rd

dam

Buffum Pond

AF Putnam Rd

Buffumville Lake

Rolling Hills Tr

Gale Rd

Dodge Ct

0.5

Miles

0

1

Whiting Rd

South Loop

▲

quarry

South Branch Little River

quarry

Potter Village Rd

TRAIL   From a yellow metal gate at the boat launch, head east into the woods on a dirt road. Turn right at a hiker sign and begin following the blue-blazed Lake Shore Trail. It's a little hard to find at first as it weaves through the disc-golf course beneath the trees, but it becomes more obvious as you go. After crossing a small wooden bridge, angle out toward the edge of the lake and then trace the shoreline. There are some rooty sections here.

At 0.3 miles the trail comes out in the open and crosses the rocky base of the dam. Then cross a grassy field, swing left, pass below a disc-golf tee, cross a concrete part of the dam, and cross a smaller grassy area before reentering the woods on the far side. Look for blue blazes on wooden posts in the open parts.

For a while the trail is wide and flat and soft beneath a canopy of pine trees. You'll begin seeing the red and white blazes of the property boundary here. Soon you arrive back at the edge of the lake. From a marker post at 0.75 miles, the Rolling Hills Trail makes a worthwhile 0.1-mile side loop around a small wooded peninsula. From there, continue winding along the shoreline of the east side of the lake, frequently rising and falling with alternating smooth stretches and rocky/rooty parts, and passing numerous rocky points and pretty, secluded coves. At about 1.25 miles, cross a small creek on a wooden bridge; a nearby post marks the Serene Inlet Path. Pass a marker for Monument Overlook on a high bluff, then drop steeply back down to the shoreline.

At 1.75 miles, cross one of the larger tributaries on a set of stepping-stone rocks. This stream may be raging in the spring yet bone-dry by late summer. At the southern end of the lake, follow the east side of a braided creek, crossing several wet spots and passing through dense riparian vegetation. A post denotes a connecting path called Side Stream Way. At one point it looks like you should bear right and cross the stream, but don't do that; the trail doesn't go that way anymore. At the very southern part of the loop, cross South Fork Little River on a wooden bridge.

Heading north from a junction on the other side, immediately cross a seepy drainage, and then climb to a ridge where there is an obscured view of the quarry operation to the west; you may hear the sound of active machinery here during the week. Overall, the trail is gentler on the west side, though there are still a lot of steep up-and-down pitches and rocky/rooty patches. At 3.8 miles, pass through an open swath and turn right onto an old road. Follow this road for the next 0.3 miles. Pass a junction with a trail leading back to the parking area, and then climb gently and reach AF Putnam Road at about 4.1 miles. Turn right and follow the path as it swings east at the junction with Oxbow Road, then cross the road at a blue arrow on the guardrail. Reenter the woods at the hiker sign on the other side and descend at a gentle grade to a junction at a post marking Causeway View. Turn left and go north along the west shore of the lake, passing several views of the beach on the other side. Shortly north of Collicum Cove, cross a new metal-railed bridge and continue north.

At the northwest side of the lake, rise a short distance along the west side of Turner Brook and then cross it on a bridge. The trail swings left/east and follows the grassy gas pipeline swath out in the open, with occasional blue-blazed wooden posts, for 0.25 miles before reentering the woods. At the northeast side of the lake, cross a sturdy metal-railed bridge over Little River. A short side path on the left leads up to a small parking area along Fulling Mill Road.

Turning right, follow the east shore of the lake south. It's flat and gentle at first, but then gets rootier and more undulating. The highest point is marked North Hill Crest; a stone bench sits beside the trail near the water's edge below. At 0.25 miles from the bench, bear left at an easy-to-miss double blue blaze (a blue-blazed trail continues straight and quickly becomes wider and more manicured before reaching the beach). Climb the slope and bear left at the picnic area to return to the parking lot.

Several miles northeast, **Hodges Village Dam** in Oxford is an ACOE project area with 22 miles of official trails (and a lot of unofficial ones), roughly divided into four main sections flanking the French River. Many of the trails are designated multi-use (shared with off-road vehicles). The four sections are: the Greenbriar Recreation Area in the northeast, the Rocky Hill Area in the southeast, the Bailey Bridge Area in the southwest, and a Multiple Use Area in the northwest (with many severely eroded trenches, extremely steep pitches, and unmarked, braided herd paths). A suggested 5- to 7-mile route for running would include a combination of blue-blazed, nonmotorized trails east of the river and orange-blazed multiuse trails on the west side, connecting via the French River pedestrian bridge in the middle. There's some particularly nice rolling singletrack sections just west of the high school north of the dam; just make sure not to veer off onto private property.

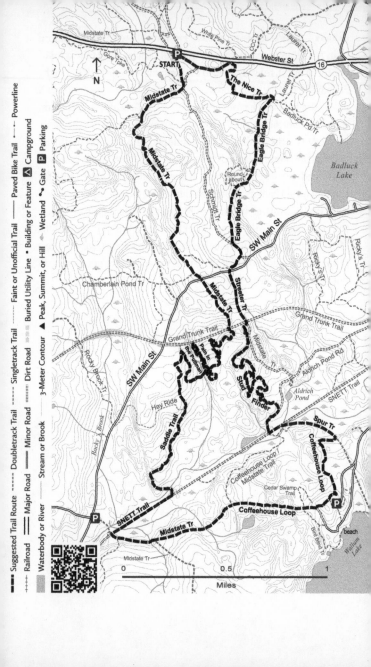

DISTANCE 10 Miles   **TOWN** Douglas
DIFFICULTY RATING Moderate   **TRAIL STYLE** Loop
TRAIL TYPE Singletrack/Doubletrack   **TOTAL ASCENT** 600 Feet

Douglas State Forest features a diverse range of trail types, including tight singletrack, wide doubletrack paths, winding dirt roads,
and straight rail trails. The singletrack trails are all well constructed
and maintained, though they don't all connect, so wider paths are
needed to link them together. The southern end of the Midstate Trail
passes through the center of this property, and it is traversed by two
of the region's long-distance rail-trail corridors. The suggested route
includes nearly all types of trail present on the property. The terrain
consists of low, dry rolling hills of oak—pine forests interspersed with
open wetlands and forested swamps. At the southern end, Wallum
Lake Park offers picnic areas, restrooms, a boat launch, and a swimming beach.

DIRECTIONS   From the center of Douglas, go 2.5 miles west on Rte.
16 to the parking area on the left. From I-395, exit 3, go east on Rte.
16 for 4.1 miles to the dirt parking area on the right; look for the
brown wooden state park sign. Alternate parking can be found at the
Wallum Lake Park portion of the site, but the road down isn't always
open and you may need to park up at the top along Wallum Lake Road.
GPS   "199 Douglas Road, Douglas, MA"

TRAIL   From the trailhead, go south on the yellow-triangle-blazed
Midstate Trail. Immediately pass an unmarked trail on the right, then
pass a trail called Gore Turnpike on the right at 0.1 miles. Stay right at
a junction with Schmidt Trail, and then at 0.2 miles continue south up

the hill on Midstate Trail. Passing numerous unmarked trails on the right, and one on the left, follow the trail over gently rolling terrain to a road at 1.5 miles. Cross the road and keep following Midstate Trail south downhill to the Grand Trunk Rail Trail. Across the rail trail and about 20 feet to the left, you'll see the trailhead for Pain in the Pullman trail.

Pullman is a narrow, winding singletrack trail that loops tightly back around on itself several times as it swoops up and down the hillside for 1.3 miles. Leaving the Midstate Trail behind, follow Pullman into the woods. Aside from a few stealthy root knobs and stony patches, the footing is excellent and the grade fairly gentle. At a junction, turn left and head south down the hill on Saddle Trail. This descent is really fun. Stay left where a barely there trail called Hay Ride leads off-property to the right. Saddle Trail crosses a stream on a wide new bridge before reaching the Southern New England Trunkline Trail (SNETT), another wide dirt rail trail.

Go right and follow the flat, easy rail trail for 0.4 miles to a 4-way intersection just past a wooden bridge. Turn left and follow the unnamed wide, rocky doubletrack trail, rising slightly to a junction with the Midstate Trail. Stay straight on Midstate Trail north (to the right, it heads south up the hill for 0.9 miles to the RI state line). In 0.5 miles you'll reach a junction where Coffeehouse Trail Loop / Midstate Trail leads left.

Stay straight and head due east on Coffeehouse Trail. In 0.4 miles, Swamp Trail leads left down the hill. This interesting quarter-mile side trail traverses a section of dark, forested cedar swamp on boardwalks. It's not great for running since the wood is often very slippery, but it's still really neat and worth checking out. Stay straight until you come out at Wallum Lake Park. In season, the park has restroom facilities, picnic areas, and a swimming beach and boat launch.

At the park, stay left at all junctions and follow Coffeehouse Loop via a series of paved and unpaved road sections past several parking areas. Eventually it dives back into the woods and reaches a wide, flat rail trail called Spur Trail. Go left on Spur and follow it for 0.4 miles back to the SNETT (staying straight at a junction where Coffeehouse leads left). Turn left on SNETT and go 0.1 miles, and then turn right on the yellow-blazed Midstate Trail and go 0.2 miles north to an easy-to-miss junction.

Turn left on Stud Finder, a narrow singletrack path that loops around for 1.2 miles on its way up to a 5-way junction at Grand Trunk Trail. The grade is gentle and the footing is good. At the 5-way junction, go north up the hill on Streeter Trail, a wide dirt road. In 0.3 miles you will reach Southwest Main Street. Across the road, bear right on an unnamed path; this trail braids, but all branches eventually head to the same place. Soon, turn left on Schmidt Trail, another wide dirt road. In a few hundred feet, bear right at a junction with Eagle Bridge Trail.

Take Eagle Bridge Trail northeast for nearly a mile around the western edge of a cedar swamp to a junction. Along the way, pass a side trail on the left called Roundabout; this purely for-the-heck-of-it path makes a really fun and fairly easy 0.3-mile extension. Turn left at an easy-to-miss junction onto TNT Trail (The Nice Trail). Take TNT 0.5 miles up to an old road just south of Rte. 16. Go left and take the dirt road back to the trailhead.

NEARBY   The Midstate Trail enters Rhode Island at the state line along the southern edge of Douglas State Forest, passes through the **Buck Hill Management Area** in the northwest corner of that state, and ends about 3.5 miles farther south on Buck Hill Road; note, however, that this section is quite rocky. Great loops are also possible on trails in the northern part of the forest, some of which continue west into Webster's **Mine Brook WMA**.

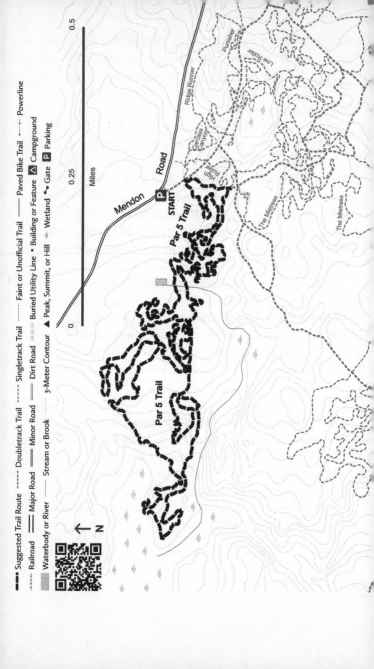

DISTANCE 4 Miles **TOWN** Sutton

DIFFICULTY RATING Moderate/Challenging **TRAIL STYLE** Loop

TRAIL TYPE Singletrack **TOTAL ASCENT** 170 Feet

Sutton State Forest features a bit of a maze of interwoven spaghetti trails, and they are not always maintained, but it's rarely crowded and to the adventurous it can be a lot of fun. The terrain is primarily gently undulating forestland. With such a complex network of unblazed trails and unmarked junctions, and only minor topographic variation throughout, it's an especially easy site to get turned around in, so make sure to have your map ready the first few times you go, or have a trails app open on your phone. Almost all the trails here feature short but steep rock-ledge pitches that may be very slippery when wet. Mountain bikers and hikers are common. The Whitinsville Water Company owns much of the land to the southeast, and it is posted.

DIRECTIONS From Rte. 146 in Sutton, take Central Turnpike 1.3 miles southwest. Turn left on Uxbridge Road and go 0.7 miles. Veer left onto Mendon Road and go 0.6 miles to the small parking area along the side of the road on the right. Look for the brown wooden trailhead kiosk sign and a metal gate.

GPS "300–412 Mendon Road, Sutton, MA"

TRAIL Starting at the kiosk, follow the dirt road past the gate into the woods. In a few hundred feet, veer right onto a wide, unmarked dirt path and cross through a stone wall (for the first of many times). The path immediately forks; go right and begin meandering up the hillside, climbing at an easy grade. Though it isn't marked here (or blazed), this is the start of the Par Five trail. For the next 3 or so miles, stay on this narrow singletrack path as it swings across the forested landscape, frequently nearly doubling back on itself but never actually crossing. There are no junctions until the end; with no intersections to concern yourself with, you can shut that part of your brain down and focus on footing and flow for a while. The terrain constantly alternates between rocks, ledges, and soft dirt.

At first, Par Five ambles around the upper part of the hillside, crossing stone walls, stony patches, and rock ledges every so often. There's quite a bit of poison ivy lining the trail in this area. The first half of the loop generally trends downhill, though there are many short uphill pitches and climbs. Near the westernmost part of the loop, about 2 miles along, the trail skirts the edge of a large open wetland and soon passes by a sign marking "Hawk's Diner." There are several muddy sections in this lower part, though rock outcroppings are still plentiful.

The second half of the loop generally trends uphill as the trail makes its way back eastward. There are several sharp switchbacks and loops along the way. At one point, the trail dips into a low area and crosses over a literal pool of poison ivy on a boardwalk; needless to say, be especially careful here. After the pool, the trail continues to zigzag around, and there's more poison ivy. There are two places in rapid succession where the trail forks briefly at what appear to be junctions; these are just braids around small ledges, and the branches soon rejoin.

At the end of the loop, drop down the side of a ledge on stone steps to a junction (the trail is marked here for anyone headed the opposite direction). Take a sharp left and follow the wide dirt path a quarter mile back up to the junction near the trailhead.

Optional Extensions You'll probably get lost, confused, or turned around when first exploring further at Sutton, but the sometimes surprisingly challenging and technical trails are worth it. One fun option is to head east downhill from the trailhead on Carcass Canyon and Ridge Runner trails and then return via Punisher and High Roller trails. A second option is to follow Low Roller as it loops crazily around the hillside southeast of the trailhead (at one point even crossing over itself) and return via Space Mountain. Other fun trails include The Mistress, Joe's Trail, Shakedown, Disneyland, Holy Roller, and TT loop.

NEARBY **Purgatory Chasm** is a small, very popular recreation area centered around a rocky ravine that can be reached from this site via a mile-long state forest road to the east. The scenic loop trail through the chasm is short and usually crowded, though a mile-long loop (Charley's Trail) rings the ravine and there's also a much less visited, even slightly overgrown 2.5-mile North Loop trail about half a mile up the road, just north of the 0.75-mile Old Purgatory Trail loop. Eight miles north of Sutton, a similarly dense maze of looping singletrack trails wind through **Colton Road Conservation Area** (a.k.a. Rayburn Trails) in Millbury. Wheeled vehicles (including bikes) are prohibited from the numerous wide, rolling trails of the **Williams Preserve** on Brigham Hill in Grafton; **Gummere Wood & Marsters Preserve** just down the hill also features a few nice twisty trails.

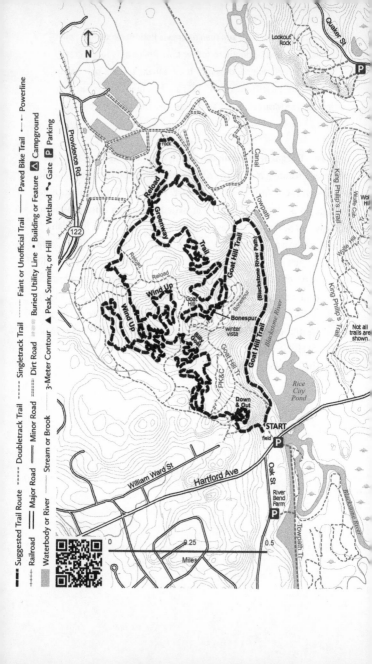

Suggested Trail Route · · · · Doubletrack Trail - - - - Singletrack Trail · · · · · · Faint or Unofficial Trail ——— Paved Bike Trail — · — Powerline

++++ Railroad ——— Major Road ===== Minor Road ===== Dirt Road ······· Buried Utility Line · Building or Feature ▲ Campground Ⓟ Parking

——— Waterbody or River ——— Stream or Brook ——— 3-Meter Contour ▲ Peak, Summit, or Hill ⚬ Wetland ⚬ Gate Ⓟ Parking

N

Quaker St.

Lookout Rock

Ⓟ

Providence Rd

122

Rock

Canal

Towpath

King Philip's Trail

Wolf Cliff

Wolfe Hill

Reload

Greenway

Trail

Goat Hill Trail

Blackstone River Path

King Philip's Trail

Reload

Reload

Wind Up

Goat Hill

Bonespur

Boneyard

winter vista

Wind Up

Goat Hill Tr.

Goat Hill Trail

Blackstone River

Not all trails are shown

PK&C

Down & Out

Rice City Pond

START

Ⓟ field

William Ward St.

Hartford Ave.

Oak St.

River Bend Farm

Ⓟ

Blackstone River

Towpath Tr.

0   0.25   0.5

Miles

DISTANCE 7.2 Miles   **TOWNS** Northbridge and Uxbridge
DIFFICULTY RATING Moderate to Challenging   **TRAIL STYLE** Loop
TRAIL TYPE Singletrack/Doubletrack   **TOTAL ASCENT** 590 Feet

Goat Hill, which is part of Blackstone River and Canal Heritage State Park, features a dense network of official and unofficial singletrack trails, only some of which are marked. A lot of trail is packed into a relatively small area surrounded by neighborhoods and the Blackstone River; this route uses most of them. There are many junctions and intersections, and navigation will be the most challenging part for first-time visitors. The wide, flat towpath paralleling the river just to the south is also a great place for beginner trail runners looking to get a sense for off-road surfaces.

DIRECTIONS   From Milford, take Rte. 16 southwest for 3.5 miles. Bear right onto Hartford Avenue and go 3 miles. Cross the Blackstone River, and the small parking area will be on the left; look for the brown wooden "Blackstone River and Canal" sign. There is extra parking just to the south at the River Bend Farm visitor center (287 Oak Street, Uxbridge).

GPS   "292 Hartford Avenue East, Uxbridge"

TRAIL   From the trailhead at the north end of the open field on the north side of Hartford Avenue, follow the wide Goat Hill Trail north along the west side of the Blackstone River for 0.7 gently rolling miles. Bear left at an unmarked junction with the Canal Towpath, then immediately left again to stay on Goat Hill Trail. The trail narrows here and gets significantly rougher. Climb at a moderately steep grade for 0.25 miles to an intersection near the top, crossing over/through a stone wall a few times but ultimately staying left of it. Stay straight where several bootleg paths cut over to a trail to the right.

At the top, take a right at an unmarked intersection with a small bare rock in the middle and begin following a winding trail (Bone Spur, not signed at this end) around the summit. Bear right at the next junction onto Greenway Trail. After passing over the summit, stay on this trail for nearly 2 miles. Stay left at several unmarked junctions with paths leading right, and descend via a series of rolling switchbacks past numerous large glacial erratic boulders to a junction by a large rock near the bottom of the north side of the hill.

Go straight at the rock, then stay left at the next two unmarked junctions. At a junction with Reload Trail, bear right onto Wind Up Trail and climb via switchbacks to a 5-way intersection.

To stay on Wind Up, bear slightly left. Follow the trail as it twists around the south side of the hill for nearly two miles. After going down several ledges (where braids in the path soon come back together again), the trail bottoms out and then climbs to and wildly winds around the upper slopes of the hill.

At another intersection with Reload, go straight and then take an immediate right on Billy Goat Trail. Descend for a mile on an extremely fun section (that comes close to crossing over itself several times) to a complicated 6-way intersection. Cross the intersection and bear left onto Down & Out Trail (the only one with a sign). Tightly wind around the upper slope of the southeast part of the hill for about 0.3 miles, ignore a steep spur called Off Ramp on the right, and then stay left at an unmarked junction (the bottom part of Off Ramp) and descend steeply back to the trailhead.

NEARBY   Immediately to the south, the wide **Blackstone River Towpath Trail** leads south for several miles along the east bank of the canal. East of Goat Hill, just across the Rice City Pond section of the Blackstone River, there's good running at the **West Hill Park** trail network. Don't miss the amazing views of Goat Hill and the river valley from graffiti-blighted **Lookout Rock**; it's accessible either by taking **King Phillip's Trail** north on the east side of the river or from a short trail off of Quaker Street. And finally, **Mendon Town Forest** about 5 miles southeast boasts its own dense network of winding singletrack; try out any of the four well-blazed color trail loops (white being the easiest and yellow the hardest).

Enticingly sinuous singletrack trail at Goat Hill in Northbridge.

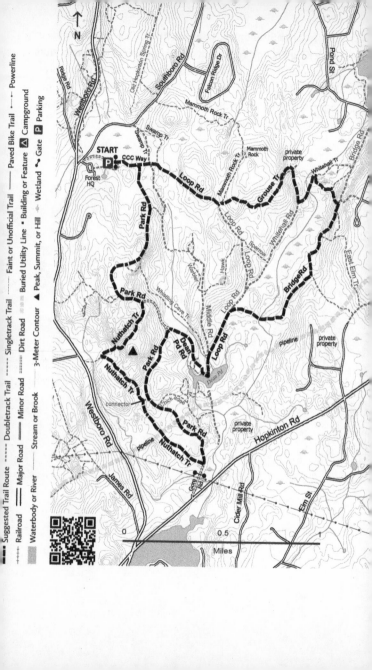

DISTANCE 6.5 Miles   **TOWNS** Upton and Hopkinton

DIFFICULTY RATING Moderate   **TRAIL STYLE** Loop

TRAIL TYPE Singletrack/Doubletrack/Dirt Road   **TOTAL ASCENT** 500 Feet

Located near the junction of the Mass Pike and I-495, Upton State Forest offers an appealing amount of forested open space close to the dense suburbs of both Boston and Worcester. The sylvan landscape of rolling hills and soggy wetlands resembles many of New England's other areas of former farms and fields, now grown over with trees and dotted with old foundations and cellar holes. This loop samples a variety of the forest's natural features and trail types, though several short side trail options to glacial erratics, boulder fields, and ponds are also worth exploring. Trail markings are fairly scarce in some areas, and many unmarked bootleg trails lead off-property onto private land, so make sure to pay careful attention to the map and obey all posted signs.

DIRECTIONS Despite being close to the Mass Pike, this site is not easy to get to from it. From I-495, exit 54B, go west on Hopkinton Road for 3.5 miles to Upton. Turn right onto Westboro Road and go 2 miles north to the state forest entrance on the right. From the center of Westborough, go south on South Street (Rte. 135) for 1 mile. Veer right onto Upton Road/Westboro Road and go south for 3.6 miles. Take a sharp left onto Park Road/CCC Way at the sign for Upton State Forest. Parking is a little funky. Pass the entrance to the bigger parking lot with the DCR lodge on the right and go 0.1 miles down Park Road/CCC Way, which can be bumpy, to a small dirt parking area. **GPS** "Park Road, Upton State Forest"

TRAIL From the parking area, follow the wide dirt track of CCC Way east. Immediately pass a trail on the right leading to the upper parking area, then go a little farther to a junction where Park Road goes up to the right. Stay straight on what is now Loop Road, passing junctions with Middle Road, Swamp Trail, and an unnamed trail on the left. At 0.6 miles from the start you'll reach a junction with the Grouse Trail on the left.

Turn left on Grouse Trail, then immediately bear right at a junction where the Mammoth Rock Trail leads straight (it's an easy quarter-mile out-and-back to the rock/ledge in question and a little network of trails to the north). Grouse Trail becomes narrow singletrack with good footing. Follow it along the east side of the hill. Stay left where a branch drops steeply down the hill and descend at a gentler grade on a switchback. At the bottom, go right at a junction on the slightly wider White Hall Road. Descend south on White Hall Road to a 3-way junction.

Take a sharp left onto Whitehall Trail, then take a sharp right onto an unmarked trail. This is a particularly pleasant section of soft, flowy singletrack. Just past a small pond on the left, turn right at a junction in a low spot. Follow the unmarked singletrack trail up to Bridge Road. Go right on Bridge Road and immediately bear right where East Elm Trail leads up to the left. Follow Bridge Road trail south just above a forested wetland to the right. At an unmarked junction, go right. Soon, stay right again at another junction. Then go about 0.25 miles down to where Bridge Road crosses the wetland on a wide wooden bridge. Then climb gently to a junction with Loop Road. Go left on Loop Road and follow it about 0.25 miles down to an intersection where Loop Road merges with Middle Road.

Optional Trim To cut out about 2.5 miles, take Whistling Cave Trail northwest from this junction. This scenic singletrack path leads past a field of large, lichen-covered glacial boulders and then up the hill at a moderate grade for 0.6 miles to a junction with Park Road near the top of the hill. At the top, go right on Park Road and follow it to the bottom. Then go left on CCC Way back to the parking area.

Stay left again and go down to the shore of Dean Pond. A complex network of singletrack trails laces the edge of the pond, but they're neither marked nor maintained. Turning around and facing the triangle junction just above the pond, go left on Dean Pond Road. Head north uphill at a gentle grade. Turn left onto Park Road at the next intersection and go almost all the way to the end, passing several marked trailheads on left (Chickadee Trail) and right (Nuthatch connector) as you descend.

Just before a gate, turn right onto Nuthatch Trail (signs say "Road," but it's a trail) and head northwest on mostly level terrain. After crossing an open pipeline corridor, bear left where a short connector trail leads back over to Park Road. After a steep climb along Nuthatch, followed by a gentle descent on the other side, take a sharp right and continue through a rocky area, and then ascend a short but steep and rugged hill. At the very end of Nuthatch, turn left on Park Road. Climb the hill, curve around to the right, and then begin descending, passing several unmarked junctions on the left and right as well as the upper end of Whistling Cave Trail on the right. Follow Park Road back down to the intersection of Loop Road and Park Road. Bear left at the intersection and head back to the parking area.

Optional Extension To add an extra 2 miles, go northwest from the parking area up to the Rabbit Run Loop trail on the west side of Ridge Road.

NEARBY Just to the northeast and directly accessible via a linking trail (Bridge Road), there is an 8-mile, yellow-blazed loop trail that rolls around the perimeter of Whitehall Reservoir in **Whitehall State Park**; combine these two sites for a moderately challenging longer run. A few miles east, **Peppercorn Hill** in Upton features a network of nice trails above Lake Maspenock. Two miles west in Grafton, the 3-mile **Warren Brook Loop Trail** is generally easy, though it can be grassy, muddy, and stony in places. Four miles north, there is a small network of variable-surface trails around **Sandra Pond** in Westborough. You can also find many miles of easy cross-country running at the **Mill Pond Trails** south of the **George H. Nichols Reservoir** in Westborough (numerous access points).

DISTANCE 3.5 Miles   TOWN Ashland
DIFFICULTY RATING Moderate   TRAIL STYLE Loop
TRAIL TYPE Singletrack/Doubletrack   TOTAL ASCENT 90 Feet

The yellow-blazed Ashland State Park Trail circles Ashland Reservoir, starting and ending at the public beach. There are several smooth, flat sections, but much of the loop undulates over rocks and roots, requiring careful attention to foot placement. While not the *easiest* site for running, it's fairly simple to navigate (follow the yellow blazes around the lake) and plenty scenic, with several swimming options along the way during the summer months. Just don't count on isolation or quiet here; it's a very popular site.

DIRECTIONS   From Hopkinton, go 3 miles northeast on Rte. 135 to State Park Road on the right. Proceed 0.4 miles east to the large paved parking lot.

GPS   "Ashland State Park Parking"

TRAIL   From the parking area, follow the paved walkway down toward the beach and look for the trailhead to the left. Follow the yellow-blazed, doubletrack-width Ashland State Park Trail / Lake Loop up into the woods. After curving to the right, descend over loose stones to the dam at the northern end of the lake. The next quarter mile or so is a flat, straight shot across the dam, including over a narrow wooden bridge at the far end.

After the dam, take a right onto singletrack trail. There may be a sign here for "Reservoir Run" trail; it's the same thing. The yellow blazes braid for the first of several times here; take the route closest to the lake for scenery and ease of navigation. For the next mile, the

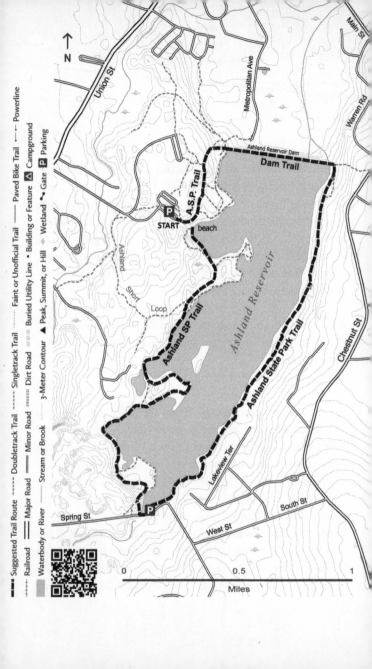

trail gently undulates up and down through the woods along the water's edge, crossing several bridges along the way.

At the southern end, turn right on Spring Street at a dirt parking area with a boat launch, cross over a bridge, and then take a right back into the woods on the other side. Follow the yellow-blazed trail north back to the beach area. This final section is slightly easier at first, but still features a number of small hills and plentiful roots. The trail braids a number of times, with yellow blazes along both options; they do come back together, so it's safe to take the scenic option next to the water on the right.

NEARBY   A few miles north, **Ashland Town Forest** and adjacent **Cowassock Woods** make an excellent site for a short to mid-distance trail run. There are no open vistas, but the forest is flecked with old quarries, abandoned cars, and many well-built bridges; also, it's well marked, and there are signs at most intersections. Combine the Red Diamond, Yellow Diamond, Purple Diamond, Blue Diamond, and Bay Circuit Trails for a 4- to 6-mile route. To the west, **Hopkinton State Park** features several easy loop options, particularly south of the reservoir; fun running paths include Long Trail, Glebe Trail, Duck Pond Trail, and Fisher Trail. A few miles south, **Wenakeening Woods** in Holliston has several miles of trail that link up with trails at Medway's **Idylbrook Recreation Area**. Last, a dense network of challenging, mostly unmarked mountain bike trails (locally known as "Vietnam") connects **Holliston Town Forest**, **Rocky Woods**, and adjacent properties.

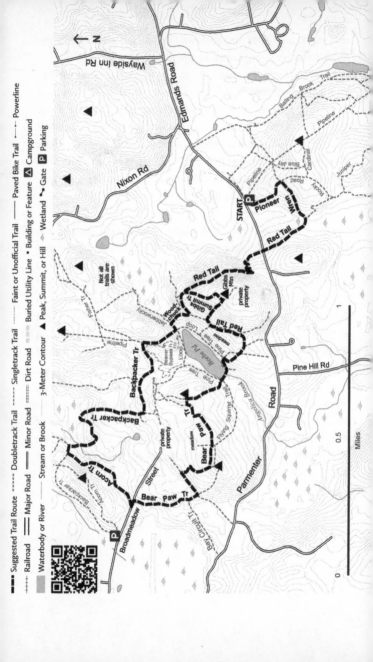

--- Suggested Trail Route ----- Doubletrack Trail ····· Singletrack Trail ----- Faint or Unofficial Trail ---- Powerline
--- Railroad === Minor Road ===== Dirt Road ···· Buried Utility Line • Building or Feature ▲ Campground
--- Waterbody or River — Stream or Brook --- 3-Meter Contour ▲ Peak, Summit, or Hill ❀ Wetland P Parking

N →

Wayside Inn Rd

Edmands Road

Nixon Rd

Pine Hill Rd

Parmenter Road

Broadmeadow Street

START

P Pioneer

Wren

Red Tail

Red Tail

Gibbs Mtn

Red Tail

Globe Summit Tr

Woods Hollow

meadow

Pine Tree Loop

Backpacker Tr

Backpacker Tr

Acorn Tr

Bear Paw Tr

Bear Paw Tr

private property

meadow

Flying Squirrel Trail

Bay Circuit Tr

Jabberwocky

Beaver Bypass

Pipeline

Fisher Tr

Not all
trails are
shown

private property

Burke Rd

Assabet Brook

Balling Brook Trail

Pipeline

Blue Jay

Cardinal

Rocky Road

Juniper

P

0   0.5   1
Miles

DISTANCE 5.2 Miles **TOWN** Framingham
DIFFICULTY RATING Moderate **TRAIL STYLE** Lollipop Loop
TRAIL TYPE Singletrack/Doubletrack **TOTAL ASCENT** 450 Feet

Callahan State Park, comprising a number of forested and open-space parcels (not all of them contiguous), provides a welcome natural respite from the surrounding development and suburbia. The park abuts a number of other conserved parcels that the trail network continues onto; the suggested route here sticks to just those within the park itself and visits many of the site's features, including ponds, fields, meadows, and hilltops. Dogs are allowed off leash in much of the southern part; many fun and relatively easy trail loops can be made there, just be prepared to encounter rambunctious off-leash dogs.

DIRECTIONS From Framingham, go northwest on Union Avenue/ Main Street/Edgell Road/Vernon Street/Grove Street for about 5 miles. Turn left onto Edmands Road and go 0.7 miles to the dirt parking area on the left. Alternate parking can be found on Broadmeadow Street on the northwest side of the route.
GPS "Callahan State Park Central Parking"

TRAIL From the trailhead, follow Pioneer Trail (the one that leads west and then immediately swings left) south up the hill at a gentle grade to Wren Trail. Turn right on Wren, then go west across and slightly down the slope. At a junction, turn right onto Red Tail Trail and follow it north up to Edmands Road. Cross Edmands Road with care. Heading north on Red Tail, climb the new switchbacks and then continue north over a shoulder of Gibbs Mountain and descend to a junction.

Continue straight down the hill on Red Tail Trail a few hundred feet, and then bear left at a junction. Bear left again at the next junction in another few hundred feet. Then take a sharp right onto Woodchuck Trail. At the bottom of the hill, turn left and go west to an open gas-pipeline corridor just above Beebe Pond.

Optional Extension Bearing slightly left, cross the pipeline corridor, and follow the Pine Tree Loop Trail into the woods next to Beebe Pond. In a few hundred feet, take a sharp right and follow the unblazed, winding singletrack Beaver Bypass trail up onto the hillside, zigzag around, and then drop back down to Pine Tree Loop. This fun trail can be hard to follow after mid-autumn. In total it will add about a mile to your run.

Turn right and go north on Woodchuck Trail along the open swath. At a junction, take a left into the woods on Backpacker Trail and go west. At a junction, turn right to stay on Backpacker Trail and then stay straight at a junction with a trail on the right. Then turn right to stay on Backpacker. Go 0.5 miles north to a junction. Turn left and go steeply up the hill a few hundred feet to a junction.

Optional Extension To add an enjoyable extra mile, continue up the slope to the next junction, then turn left onto the upper part of Acorn Trail. Follow Acorn southwest to the parking lot, then bear right and reenter the woods at the trailhead kiosk. Follow Backpacker Trail 0.4 miles northeast back to the junction with upper Acorn.

Take a left on Acorn Trail and go south to Broadmeadow Street. Go left on the road, then turn right onto Bear-Paw Trail and follow it for about a mile back to Beebe Pond. To do so, stay straight at a junction where the Bay Circuit Trail (BCT) leads right. Go a few hundred feet to an intersection with an old road. Take a left to stay on Bear-Paw Trail. Then turn right and climb briefly. Curve right, then turn left at a junction and go to the edge of an open field. Follow Bear-Paw Trail east along the southern edge of the field, staying straight at a junction and passing through a stone wall. Near the eastern end of the field, turn right into the woods at one junction and go a few feet to another. Turn right and descend to the southern end of Beebe Pond, passing an old chimney just before the bottom.

Cross an old dam at the edge of the pond on Pine Tree Loop, then stay straight at an intersection. Climb briefly to another junction and then take a sharp right. Climb out into Beebe Meadow and stay straight at an intersection. Staying left at several junctions with paths leading right, trace the upper edge of the open meadow on Red Tail Trail, then reenter the woods and take a left. Go straight at an immediate junction, then turn right on Gibbs Summit trail. Turn left at the top, cross over the wooded summit, and descend to a junction. This is the end of the loop portion of the route. Finish by going right and returning back to the trailhead the way you came.

> *Optional Extension(s)* To add on a fun extra loop (or loops) on mostly easy to moderate trails, head south from the parking area Pipeline Trail, Rocky Road, or Red Tail Trail and explore the dense network near Eagle Pond. A loop combining the Earthen Dam, Coco Ridge, and Rocky Road Trails is also nice. Dogs are allowed off leash here.

NEARBY Southwest of Callahan and linked by the BCT, the **Sudbury Reservoir Watershed** in Marlborough features numerous trails, including the still-in-development 33-mile **Boroughs Loop Trail**. An undulating network of nice, well-marked trails at **Nobscot Hill** and **Tippling Rock** in Framingham/Sudbury can be accessed from parking areas on Rte. 20 or Brimstone Lane.

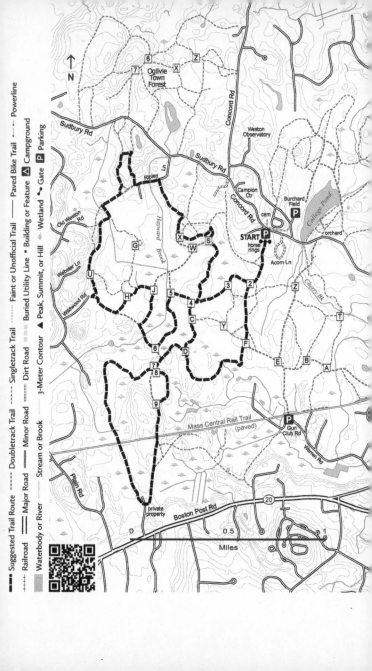

DISTANCE 6.2 Miles **TOWN** Weston
DIFFICULTY RATING Easy **TRAIL STYLE** Loop
TRAIL TYPE Singletrack/Doubletrack **TOTAL ASCENT** 170 Feet

Jericho Town Forest in Weston offers some of the easiest, most serene trail running around. There are no big hills and far fewer rocks and roots than at most other sites. Overall, the trails are remarkably smooth and gentle. Some of the junctions (but not all) are designated and marked with numbers or letters. All trails are marked with green W and conifer-tree symbols. On the east side, Jericho directly abuts Fiske Town Forest, and the trail network is shared by the two with no noticeable boundary or change on the ground. A paved rail trail cuts through several parts of the very southern edge of the forest. This route roughly follows the course of an annual trail race here; it's convoluted, but it visits many of the nicer trails while generally avoiding overly wet and other problem areas. Also, it adds up to an almost perfect 10K distance.

DIRECTIONS From Boston Post Road just north of Rte. 20 in the village of Weston, go northwest on Concord Road for 1.4 miles. The small dirt parking area is on the left. There is a sign for Ruth B. Dickson Memorial Field. Alternately, there is a large parking lot at the Weston College Land recreation area north of Concord Road, with an unmarked trail link. There's also a limited amount of parking along Warren Avenue on the south side.

GPS "Weston Wayland Horse Show"

TRAIL Starting at the northern trailhead, follow the wide path south along the edge of the field, keeping the horse rings to your right. At the first junction, bear left into the woods. Keep heading south on the wide path, passing trails coming in from the right and then the left. At 0.25 miles from the start, turn right at junction (jct.) 2. Go west to jct. 3. Bear right and go west to a junction, just before reaching jct. 4.

Take a sharp right and go north on a narrower trail to jct. S. Turn right and go a few hundred feet to another junction, just before descending steeply down the slope. Take a sharp left and climb the narrow singletrack trail up and over a small hill, passing a rock cairn and side trail on the right, to intersection X. At X, go straight, passing trails on the left and then the right. At the next junction, turn left and go across the slope to Ripley Lane.

Turn left and go a few hundred feet west on Ripley. Where the road swings left, stay straight on doubletrack trail and then take the first right on singletrack. Go north up the hill. Just before dipping down and crossing a brook, turn left and go a few hundred feet west. Take another left and go south. Bear right at a fork and descend briefly to a junction. Bear right back onto the doubletrack and go west along the lane to a junction just before some boardwalks. Go left and follow the trail south a few hundred feet along the edge of a field. At a junction, take a right and rise a few hundred feet to a junction. Bear left and go to a junction. Bear left again and go to jct. U. Stay straight and go to the end of the trail at the Wildwood Road cul-de-sac.

From Wildwood, go back into the woods by taking a sharp left. Bear left at a triangle junction, then stay right at the next three junctions (including H and J). At the next junction, turn left and go southeast across the wide causeway over Hayward Brook to jct. 6. From here, make a wide loop around the wetland by going left and then staying right at the next three junctions (5, 4, and C) for 0.5 miles to jct. D. There is one low, wet, grassy area in this section.

At D, begin a lollipop loop by taking a right and going west/south to a junction. Bear left and go a few hundred feet to jct. 7; this is the start of the loop portion. Immediately take a left at 8 and climb the hill on singletrack. Go 0.2 roller-coastery miles to jct. 9; this is the most technical part of the route. Turn left and follow the wide path south to the paved rail trail beneath the power line. Stay left of the metal power-line tower. Passing a trail leading down to the left, go right at the next junction and quickly reach a private driveway. Bearing slightly right, cross the driveway and follow the trail north back to the rail trail. Cross the rail trail and go north and then east to close the loop. Turn left at jct. 7 and follow the lollipop stick back to jct. D.

Back at D, turn right and wind around to jct. F; this section gently rolls over some low hills and crosses a few boardwalks. Turn left at F and follow the wide main path almost due north back to the parking lot, passing several junctions and intersections along the way.

NEARBY   The trails in the eastern part of this site are also excellent for running, though at present there's at least one dodgy stream crossing. Immediately to the north across Concord Road from the Weston Wayland parking lot and directly linkable by trail, **Weston College Land** has an easy 3-mile loop trail; its trail network also runs along the shore of **College Pond** and through a small open orchard. Also connected to Jericho by trail, the **Ogilvie Town Forest** just to the northwest has a smaller network of more challenging trails, some of which go over and around sizable hills. Several miles northeast, **Cat Rock Park** in Weston is a small open-space area with some good trails at an old ski hill (but parking is for town residents only on weekends).

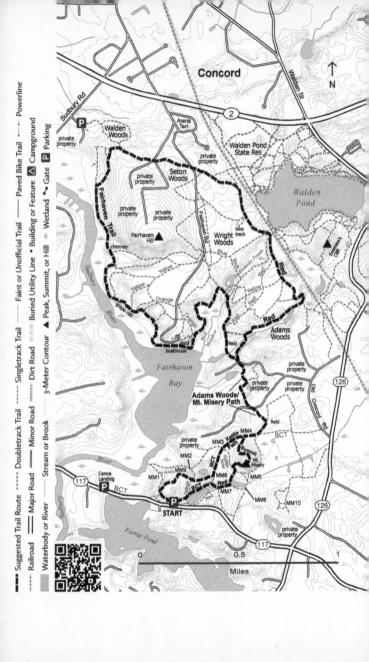

Suggested Trail Route | ----- Doubletrack Trail | ----- Singletrack Trail | .... Faint or Unofficial Trail | ---- Paved Bike Trail | -·- Powerline
Railroad | ==== Major Road | ==== Minor Road | ::::::: Dirt Road | ▄▄▄▄ Buried Utility Line | • Building or Feature | ▲ Campground
Waterbody or River | —— Stream or Brook | ---- 3-Meter Contour | ▲ Peak, Summit, or Hill | ⚬ Wetland | ⌐ Gate | P Parking

DISTANCE 6.5 Miles   **TOWNS** Concord and Lincoln
DIFFICULTY RATING Moderate   **TRAIL STYLE** Figure-8 Loop
TRAIL TYPE Singletrack/Doubletrack   **TOTAL ASCENT** 410 Feet

Mount Misery is a relatively small, forested hill, but it anchors the largest conservation area in Lincoln and abuts many other open-space properties, including Walden Pond, Wright Woods, Adams Woods, and Walden Woods Project land, all of which are connected by an extensive trail network. Part of the Bay Circuit Trail runs through the site. This route connects several of the properties and offers a sampling of their many trails. Some junctions are marked, but not all. Some portions of trail along the banks of the Sudbury River are subject to seasonal flooding and should be bypassed with high-water routes. There is a small alternate parking area along Sudbury Road in Concord.

DIRECTIONS The main parking lot is on the north side of Rte. 117 in Lincoln, about 0.6 miles east of the Sudbury River bridge; look for a brown wooden "Mount Misery Conservation Land" sign. An overflow parking lot is located at the canoe landing 0.5 miles to the west, near the Sudbury River bridge.
GPS "Mount Misery Parking Lot, Lincoln"

TRAIL Starting at the dirt parking area, head northeast on the Bay Circuit Trail. Pass a pond on your right, and then go right on a red-blazed trail at the far end. Drop to a bridge, then climb steeply to junction MM7. Go left on the yellow-blazed trail, then take another left at the next intersection. Pass another pond on the right and then climb to an intersection.

Bearing slightly left, cross the Kettlehole Trail and climb steeply up the south side of 262-foot Mount Misery. Cross the forested summit, then descend at a gentle grade down the north side. At a junction, go right on the wide path. At the edge of a field, bear left and follow the path along the western edge. At the next junction, bear left into the woods on the Adams Woods / Mount Misery Path. Follow this trail north past several fields and across two paved roads.

Just north of the second road, bear right at a junction and descend the hillside to another junction. You are now in Adams Woods. Go right and follow the red-blazed trail northeast to a junction. Turn left and climb steeply uphill via a switchback on the red-blazed trail. Railroad tracks will be on your right. At the top, stay right on the red trail. Heading northwest, stay straight at several junctions until you reach a major intersection (where you can just barely see part of Walden Pond across railroad tracks to the northeast; an unofficial trail crosses over the live tracks to the pond). The boggy Andromeda Ponds kettleholes are down to the left.

Bearing slightly left, enter Wright Woods. Take the trail closest to the tracks northwest up the short hill, then turn right and stay on this main doubletrack path at several junctions where trails lead right. At a paved (private) road crossing, start following white markers inside red circles. Cross two more paved roads, then take a left just after crossing into Walden Woods Project land and descend Fairhaven Hill. Bear left at the bottom on the unsigned Fairhaven Trail.

Follow Fairhaven Trail, occasionally marked with white discs, south along the east side of the Sudbury River. Pass an old chimney and stay right at all junctions. The next section floods seasonally, so use the orange-blazed high-water route at those times. With the river on your right, pass by a house and a boathouse and beneath an overlook on the bluff above. Curve left around a wet meadow, again staying right at all junctions. The Fairhaven Trail ends at the southern end of Andromeda Ponds. Staying right at three junctions, follow the red-blazed trail through Adams Woods to a junction.

Bear right and pass through a wooden gate. Cross Pleasant Meadow on a narrow singletrack path, then bear right on the Adams Woods / Mount Misery Path after reentering the woods on the other side. Return toward Mount Misery the way you came in. Back at the north side of Mount Misery, take Kettle Path west. At intersection MM3, stay straight. At MM8, bear right and climb the low ridge. Cross over a yellow-blazed path, then bear left at MM9 and descend the hill. Turn left at the bottom to return to the trailhead.

NEARBY A 4-mile loop rings **Sandy Pond** (a.k.a. **Flint's Pond**) and the deCordova museum, mostly on **Lincoln Town Trails**, though it isn't specifically marked and there are two paved road crossings at the southern end. The historic **Battle Road** at **Minute Man National Historical Park** in Lexington/Concord is a wide, easy, gently undulating 5-mile trail with narrower side trails at Fiske Hill and Gowings Swamp at either end. To the north, **Estabrook Woods** and adjacent forested properties in southern Carlisle feature sprawling, interconnected networks of (mostly unmarked) trails. About 8 miles due west, **Stow Town Forest** features several color-coded trails that are well marked and well blazed, mostly on soft dirt with pine needles; access from Bradley Lane in Stow. The flat, well-maintained trails at **Assabet River National Wildlife Refuge** are also an option in Stow/Maynard, though parts are sometimes flooded.

WALDEN POND No outdoorsy person's time in Massachusetts is complete without a pilgrimage to Walden Pond, so it'd be tempting to combine yours with a workout. But the main 1.7-mile loop around it, the Pond Path, is specifically closed to running, and many of the parallel trails slightly above aren't especially great for running (rooty with a lot of braids). Nevertheless, you can stage a number of fun runs from here if you venture beyond the beaten path and include side loops over Emerson's Cliff and the Esker Trail or through the adjacent conservation properties. There is a fee for parking.

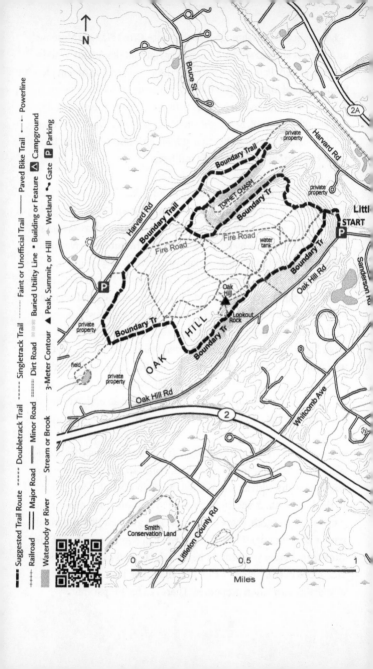

DISTANCE 3.4 Miles   **TOWN** Littleton
DIFFICULTY RATING Moderate   **TRAIL STYLE** Lollipop Loop
TRAIL TYPE Singletrack/Doubletrack   **TOTAL ASCENT** 325 Feet

Capping the northern end of Shrewsbury Ridge, Oak Hill features a fun network of well-marked trails along with a variety of interesting natural features, including Tophet Chasm (a wooded wetland flanked by steep side walls) and Lookout Rock (a 475-foot-high scenic vista on the east side of the hill). There are more than 7 miles of trail total, all packed into a relatively small area. This route follows the yellow-blazed Boundary Trail more or less around the perimeter; the loop portion makes an almost perfect 5K distance. There is another convenient trailhead and parking area along Harvard Road.

DIRECTIONS   From I-495, exit 79, take Rte. 2A west for 0.2 miles to Littleton. Turn left onto King Street, and then go straight at the intersection onto Sanderson Road. Turn right on Oak Hill Road and go 0.1 miles to the small dirt lot by the trailhead on the right, marked with a brown wooden sign.

GPS   "Oak Hill Reservation Lookout Rock Trailhead"

TRAIL   Starting at the trailhead, follow the wide dirt path up the hill. It braids twice but comes back together each time. At an intersection, go right and begin following the yellow-blazed Boundary Trail loop counterclockwise across the hillside. There are many junctions with orange-, blue-, and red-blazed trails along the way; stay on the Boundary Trail at all of them.

The trail traverses the rim of a long, deep cleft in the hill called Tophet Chasm. An interesting orange-blazed trail leads through it along the edge of Tophet Swamp at the bottom, but the trail is frequently wet and slippery. After nearly circling the chasm, the trail swings sharply left at the northernmost part of the loop; an orange-blazed side trail leads down to a gate along Harvard Road.

The trail then runs southeast along the property line above Harvard Road. Go left at a junction where a path leads west to the Harvard Road parking area. Continue south, then bear left and climb east up the ridge at a steady grade. You'll pass an orange-blazed spur trail leading to a scenic pond on the right and then pass several trails on the left. After cresting the ridge, the trail snakes along the eastern side of the hill to Lookout Rock ledge, where there is a panoramic southeast view. From there, the trail drops northeast down the hill at a gentle grade back toward the trailhead, crossing over several unmarked paths and old roads along the way.

NEARBY   Several miles to the south, a number of small, well-marked, and fun-to-run loops can be strung together at the **Patch Hill Conservation Area** in Boxborough; park at Liberty Field or a small roadside pull-off about half a mile south. To the east, a complicated but enjoyable 6-ish-mile run can be made by linking together the four yellow-blazed loops at the adjacent conservation properties of **Spring Hill**, **Nashoba Brook**, **Camp Acton**, and **Robbins Mill** in Acton; each site has its own parking and access. Just west of there (still in Acton), shortish (1- to 2-mile) yellow- and blue-blazed loops can be combined at **Nagog Hill** (smooth trails) and **Grassy Pond** (stony trails) conservation areas; just north of there, Littleton's hilly **Sarah Doublet Forest** features several short but runnable loops (connectable to **Nagog Hill Orchard** and **Cobbs Woods** to the north). **Long Lake Park** features several scenic loops in the woods south of the lake. South of Rte. 2 in Acton, **Great Hill** has a rolling 2-mile trail around it as well as steeper trails going over the wooded top. To the north, **Lowell-Dracut-Tyngsboro State Forest** also has several mid-distance loop options.

DISTANCE 6 Miles   **TOWN** Carlisle

DIFFICULTY RATING Easy/Moderate   **TRAIL STYLE** Loop

TRAIL TYPE Singletrack/Doubletrack   **TOTAL ASCENT** 300 Feet

With more than 20 miles of trails through open fields, forested swamps, and rocky woodlands, this site makes a great destination for runners of all abilities. The park is centered around a working dairy farm, and trails encircle both the farm and several active agricultural fields. It's a popular place, and some of the trails are also open to horseback riders, mountain bikers, and dog walkers. This loop includes a number of the more challenging trails on the property, but beginners or runners seeking only easy trails can find plenty of tame and gentle loop options here as well. Many of the easier loops are on wide, rolling cross-country-style trails that are sometimes even grassy, while most of the forested singletrack trails are hillier and rockier. Bonus: if it's a hot day and the concession stand is open, you can get a post-run ice cream right on site.

DIRECTIONS From I-495, exit 88, take Rte. 110 south for 0.5 miles. Go south on Rte. 4 for 1.1 miles. Bear right onto Concord Road and go 2.1 miles south. Just past Great Brook Ski Touring Center, turn left on North Road and go 0.2 miles east to the parking area on the left. From Rte. 128, exit 49B, go 7 miles northwest on Rte. 225 to the center of Carlisle. Turn right on Lowell Road and go 2 miles north. Turn right on North Road and go 0.2 miles east to the parking area on the left. There's alternate parking at a smaller lot slightly farther east on North Road and seasonally (spring–fall) at the ski touring center along Lowell Road. Parking fees apply at all locations.

GPS "Great Brook Farm State Park, 300 North Road"

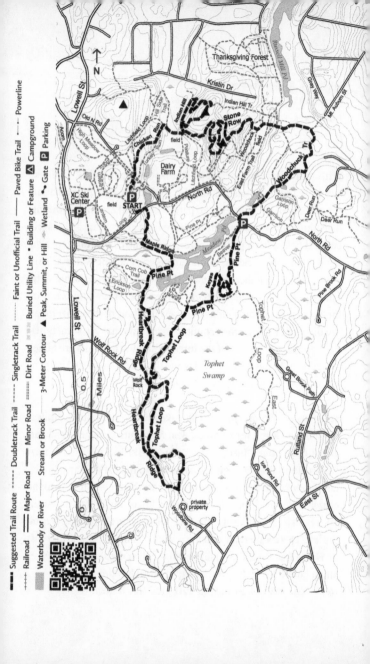

TRAIL   At the south end of the parking area, follow an unmarked path southeast, with the pond on your left. Immediately cross North Road (paved) and follow the unsigned sandy path through stone-flecked woods, passing by a wetland on the right; there are occasional blue marker blazes. You'll soon reach the wide, flat Maple Ridge Trail.

Go left on Maple Ridge and follow it to a junction. A marshy cove of Meadow Pond is visible out in front of you. Bear right onto the wide, yellow-blazed Pine Point Loop trail. Go south, cross a stream on a wide stone bridge, and climb a gentle slope to the first junction with Erickson Loop on the right. Continue straight, passing the field, Corn Cob Trail, and a vernal pool on the right, to a second junction with Erickson Loop (which makes a nice half-mile extension).

Bearing slightly left, continue heading south on Pine Point Loop trail to a junction. Take a right on the white-blazed Heartbreak Ridge trail and immediately begin climbing the low ridge. The trail immediately gets narrower and rockier here. Go south to a junction just past a large split boulder. Bear left and go a few feet to a 4-way intersection. Stay right and continue south for 0.5 miles; the footing becomes notably gentler for this next stretch.

At a fork, take a sharp left onto Tophet Loop West trail. Follow this white-blazed trail north as it winds past Tophet Swamp on the right. This trail has well-graded inclines and curves around the contours of the landscape, and there are several wooden boardwalk bridges. In 0.5 miles you'll arrive back at an intersection with Heartbreak Ridge trail. Veer right down the hill and stay on Tophet Loop until you arrive at an intersection.

Turn right onto Pine Point Loop trail. Just past a cove of Meadow Pond, take a left onto Keyes Loop trail. Keyes Loop curves back and forth through stones and stone walls in a pine woodland until it rejoins Pine Point Loop. Go left on Pine Point and head north, passing junctions with Beaver Loop on the left, to a gate at a small dirt parking area.

Cross the paved road and go through the gate on the other side. Go north on Woodchuck trail, staying straight at junctions with Garrison Loop and Deer Run (both fun trails), and several connector trails on the left. Stay straight at jct. 10 and cross a wooden bridge over a brook. After passing a few unmarked junctions for trails leading north to Thanksgiving Forest on the right, you'll soon arrive at a junction (jct. 8) with East Farm Trail near the northwest corner of a small cornfield. Bear right to stay on Woodchuck.

Soon after reentering the woods, turn right at a sign with an arrow onto the red-blazed Stone Row trail, which is somewhat technical, with a lot of rocks. A bit of fancy footwork is required; it's not all rocks, though, and it is runnable the whole way. After immediately rising to an unmarked junction with a faint trail leading down to the right, Stone Row bears left and winds its way up the hill at an easy grade. About a quarter mile along, stay left where a shortcut path leads down straight ahead. Soon you'll reach the top of the hill and begin descending. At an unmarked junction, go right and then quickly right again at a second unmarked junction. Climb another hill and then wind around and descend a series of stone steps to a marked intersection.

Take a hard right and climb the east side of the red-blazed Indian Hill Trail. Cross over the top, pass a trail leading down to the right, and then descend via a series of gently sloping switchbacks. The footing is excellent here. Stay left at a junction and drop back to the start of Indian Hill Trail. Taking a right onto Litchfield Loop, go around the edge of a field. At a junction, three options all lead back to the barns and pastures of the central farm complex. The rest of Litchfield Loop is the longest and easiest route; Chicken Run trail is slightly shorter, narrower, and rougher; Turkey Run trail is shortest, but also narrowest and most rugged.

NEARBY   Several adjacent sites can be reached by connector trails, including a 1-mile loop at **Thanksgiving Forest** just north across the town line in Chelmsford and a trio of short loops of the Acorn Trail on the west side of Lowell Road. About a mile to the west, wide gravel trails run through and around the working wetlands of **Carlisle Cranberry Bog**, which also features a narrower, unmarked Peninsula Trail through flat woods. Thanks to NEMBA, the dense network of beautifully built and well-maintained trails at Chelmsford's **Russell Mill Pond & Town Forest** about two miles to the northeast of the park packs a lot of path into a relatively small area. Just east of Rte. 3, **Billerica State Forest** features a similarly switchbacky web of trails; these are very popular with mountain bikers. Seven miles northwest, a 3- to 5-mile run can be made at **Stony Brook Conservation Land** in Westford by combining the Waki, Stony Brook, and Burge's Pond Trails (access from Depot Street).

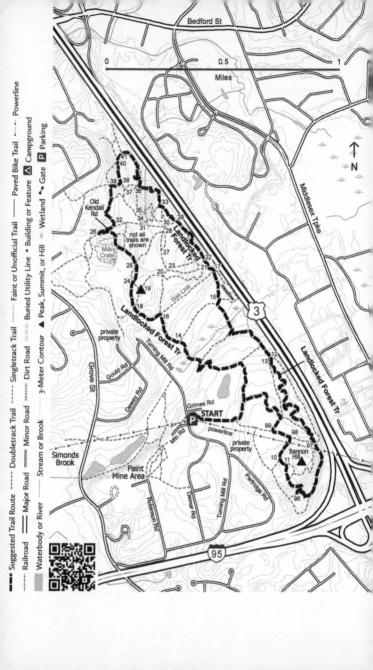

DISTANCE 4.6 Miles   **TOWN** Burlington
DIFFICULTY RATING Moderate   **TRAIL STYLE** Loop
TRAIL TYPE Singletrack   **TOTAL ASCENT** 350 Feet

Despite being directly bordered on all sides by busy highways and suburban neighborhoods, Burlington's Landlocked Forest nevertheless frequently feels remote, off the beaten path, and not as noisy as you'd think. The Landlocked Forest Loop trail, marked with yellow arrows in white circles, is a very fun, rolling 4-ish-mile lollipop-loop route. Several wet sections in the middle have recently been rerouted over gorgeous boardwalks. There are many other smaller, color-coded trail loops and (sometimes unmapped) sinuous singletrack sections for adding extra mileage, but in general navigation is fairly easy; just follow yellow arrows the whole way. The footing varies widely, from smooth and soft to rocky and rooty. Check the Friends of Burlington Landlocked Forest website for current information and updates.

DIRECTIONS   From I-95, exit 49B, go 0.3 miles north on Rte. 4. Turn right on Eldred Street and go 0.5 miles. Turn left on Grove Street and go 0.4 miles. Turn right on Gould Road and go 0.3 miles. Turn right on Turning Mill Road and go 0.3 miles. There is roadside parking beneath the power lines; look for the wooden trailhead kiosk.

From Rte. 3, exit 73, go 1 mile west on Rte. 63 then 1.2 miles south on Page/Grove Street to Gould/Turning Mill, then follow as noted above.
GPS   "Burlington Landlocked Forest"

TRAIL   From the info kiosk at the parking area, go due east on the stony dirt road under the power lines. Bear left into the woods at the second junction (jct.), following the occasional orange markers of the entrance path. After a short rise, turn right at the first junction and begin following the yellow arrows of the Landlocked Forest Loop trail counterclockwise (all the way back to this junction, miles later).

Turn right at the next junction, and then head south, concurrent with the blue arrows of Bannon Hill Loop. Turn left at jct. 99 and follow the power line east to jct. 98. Turn right and begin circling Bannon Hill. Bear left at jct. 10, then right at jct. 11, and then descend switchbacks to a left turn at jct. 96. Still descending, pass a large boulder and then head north back up to jct. 97 at the power lines.

Head north back into the woods and bear right at a junction where the blue loop goes left. Turn right at jct. 13 and then immediately left at jct. 12. Now coincident with the green-blazed Aquifer Loop and staying left at an unmarked junction, descend to a long boardwalk crossing of a forested wetland. Turn right away from the green loop, then left at jct. 15. Cross a small meadowy spot and continue straight at jct. 17.

Continue trending northwest on the yellow loop at the next several marked and unmarked junctions to where the trail swings left at the northern end of the property. You'll also pass a spur branch to a brief scenic vista of Rte. 3 on the right along the way.

Now heading south from jct. 41, keep following the yellow loop as it climbs to Old Kendall Road at jct. 32. Turn right and climb a bit more, coincident now with the red loop, and then turn left at jct. 26.

Optional Extension(s)   Of the various unmarked singletrack trails at this site, one of the most fun to run is a sinuous, hilly half-mile gem called Milk Crate; it starts at a milk crate (soon after jct. 26). Nearby, the quarter-mile Switchbacks trail just north of the red loop is also enjoyable.

Continuing south, stay on the yellow loop at the next several marked and unmarked junctions. You'll leave the red loop at jct. 16, descend and rejoin the green loop at jct. 14, cross another swamp boardwalk, and then climb switchbacks to a junction at a stone wall. Turn left at the wall, then right, and then gradually climb back to the close of the yellow loop. Return to the trailhead the way you came in.

NEARBY   Just west across the street, **Paint Mine** and **Simond's Brook** conservation areas offer 2–3 more miles of boardwalky trail. Several miles northeast, rooty trails at **Mill Pond Conservation Area** in Burlington wind about through woodlands, under power lines, and sometimes even across bare ledges; parking is limited. South of Rte. 128, **Mary Cummings Park** and adjacent **Whispering Hill Woods** in Burlington support a small but very runnable system of rolling, well-signed trails through woods and fields (this is a great site for first-time trail runners).

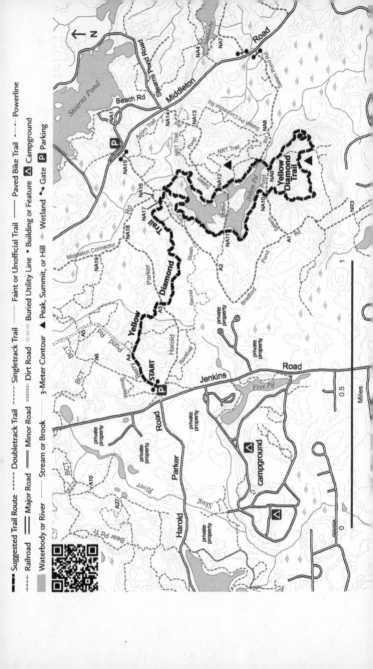

DISTANCE 4.5 Miles

TOWNS Andover, North Andover, North Reading, and Middleton

DIFFICULTY RATING Moderate/Challenging   **TRAIL STYLE** Lollipop Loop

TRAIL TYPE Singletrack   **TOTAL ASCENT** 250 Feet

Harold Parker State Forest covers a huge wooded area north of Boston. The forest's thousands of acres of rolling hills are dotted with swamps, vernal pools, and dammed ponds. Big glacial erratic boulders are common throughout. The property is densely laced with a wide variety of trails that could be explored for days without ever repeating the same sections. There are many intersecting and crisscrossing trails, both marked and unmarked. The Bay Circuit Trail winds through the northern part of the forest and passes near Berry Pond. The route options are almost endless, and it's easy to string together a long trail run of 20 or 30 miles. Loops and sections can be accessed from several different trailheads and parking areas. This route follows yellow diamond markers the whole way and makes a great introduction, but it's only one of many terrific run options here. Other particularly fun trails to seek out and explore at Harold Parker include Oak Tree Hill, Delano Pond, Suffering, Field Pond, NRT South and North, Acorn, Lock & Load, and Black Ops. The loops directly around the shorelines of Brackett and Fields Ponds are a little rough and rooty for running.

DIRECTIONS From I-93, exit 35, take Rte. 125 northeast for 2.5 miles. Turn right on Harold Parker Road and go 1.5 miles through the forest to the parking area (fee) on the east side of Jenkins Road, a few hundred feet past the small brown Harold Parker State Forest sign.

GPS "Parker Parking, Andover"

TRAIL Starting from Gate 13 at the Jenkins Road lot, follow Berry Pond Road northeast gently uphill for nearly a quarter mile to a junction at A4. Turn right onto the yellow-blazed Yellow Diamond Trail (YDT), a winding, rocky singletrack path. After passing an old dynamite storage shed and an unmarked trail on the right, cross over Harold Parker Road at A3. Go east on YDT for a half mile, passing an unmarked trail on the right, to Bradford Pond Road (a fire road) at NA17. Cross the road, pass a faint unmarked trail on the right, and reach a junction that marks the start of the Salem Pond Loop where yellow blazes lead both ways. It's 1 mile to this point.

To do the loop clockwise, bear left and descend to an unmarked junction. Go right and follow YDT around the north and east sides of Salem Pond to NA12 at Upper Salem Pond Road. Cross the road and continue following the trail above the east side of Salem Pond to Salem Pond Road. Turn right and follow the road across a bridge at the southern end of the pond, then turn sharply left onto "Terry Trail" at NA9. Follow the fun, winding singletrack around the hill to NA10 higher up on Salem Pond Road. Cross the fire road and follow the YDT around the west side of Salem Pond to NA11. Cross the road and follow YDT back to the start of the loop.

Optional Alternate Return From the Salem Pond loop, it is possible to return back to the Jenkins Road lot via a set of unmarked trails ("Secret Stash" and "Rootball") that roughly parallel the YDT heading west. These fun trails bear left off the YDT at an easy-to-miss unmarked junction about 100 feet west from the loop junction (before crossing Bradford Pond Road).

NEARBY There are very enjoyable trail networks a few miles to the west at **Goldsmith Reservation** in Andover, at **Boxford State Forest** a few miles to the east, and at **Wildcat Forest** about 8 miles northeast in Boxford. Dogs can run free at **Reading Town Forest**'s small trail network.

DISTANCE 5 Miles   **TOWNS** Andover and North Andover

DIFFICULTY RATING Moderate   **TRAIL STYLE** Loop

TRAIL TYPE Singletrack/Doubletrack   **TOTAL ASCENT** 475 Feet

With nearly 15 miles of trails and countless mix-and-match loop options, Ward Reservation makes an excellent destination for rewarding trail runs of any length or difficulty. The landscape is dominated by two medium-size hills, Holt Hill and Boston Hill, but there are also scenic woods, swamps, bogs, meadows, and rolling fields throughout. This route roughly circles the main part of the property and visits many of the more interesting features. However, all of the side trails mentioned are worth exploring, and the fields to the south make for spectacular open-air cross-country running. The Bay Circuit Trail (BCT) passes through the southwestern side of the property. There is a small fee to park in the main lot, but the site can also be accessed from a number of side trails.

DIRECTIONS   From I-93, exit 35, take Rte. 125 north for 5 miles to Prospect Road. Turn right and go 0.3 miles to the entrance and parking on right, marked by a Trustees signpost. From I-495, exit 100A, take Rte. 114 east for 1.7 miles. Turn right onto Rte. 125 and go 1.6 miles south. Turn left onto Prospect Road; continue as above.

GPS   "Ward Reservation, Prospect Road"

TRAIL   From the parking area, follow the accessible entrance path downhill into the woods. At the first junction (jct.), go left and climb the switchback, following yellow and red blazes. At the paved road, look for a sign for Rachel's Trail. Follow this red-blazed dirt path up the hill above a driveway below on the right. The path traces the lower

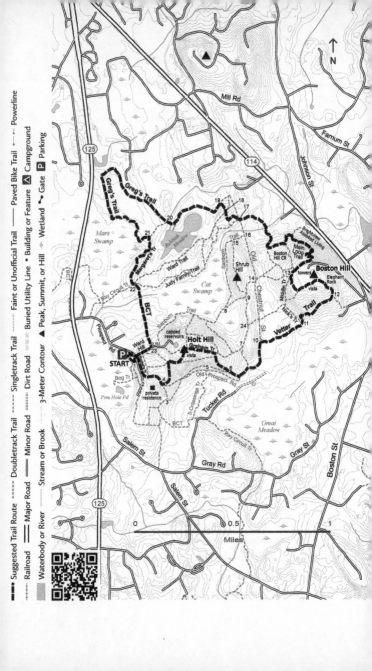

end of an open field, rising to a junction. Stay straight and follow the now red and yellow blazes up through flanking trees to a junction (4) with a view out across open fields. Bearing left, follow the wide, yellow-blazed dirt path up Holt Hill. This section coincides with a segment of the Bay Circuit Trail. The path climbs through forest, swings right at an unmarked junction, and then curves left as it climbs though an open field to the top.

The top of Holt Hill is marked by a wheel of rocks called the Solstice Stones. On a clear day, you can see the skyline of Boston to the south. From here, follow the blue-blazed Graham Trail east down the hill. At the first junction, bear right and drop at a steep grade to a junction, passing an unmarked junction and a junction (6) with Church Trail on the right along the way. Following red and blue blazes, take Old Prospect Road left/east. Pass an unmarked trail on the left, then bear left at Old Chestnut Street and go north to jct. 10.

Turn right on the blue-blazed Vetter Trail and go east, cross a wooden bridge over a low area, and reach jct. 11 where Nick's Trail leads left. Stay straight and climb Boston Hill via a series of swooping curves. This "barrens" section is heavily managed with clearing and fire and features an almost savanna-like feel. After passing jct. 12 and Elephant Rock on the right, bear left across the hilltop to a set of Adirondack chairs at a vista on the left.

From the vista, follow blue-blazed Elephant Rock Trail back into the woods. Stay right at a junction with Middle Trail and cross onto the Boston Hill CR (Conservation Restriction) property. Pass a junction on the left, keeping a chain-link fence on the right, and then reach the concrete remains of the top of an old ski lift on the left. From there, follow the arrows of Main Loop Trail down a series of switchbacks through overgrown old ski trails; with smooth curves and well-constructed boardwalks, this stretch is ridiculously fun to run. After passing a trail leading off-property down to the right and then reclimbing the hill a bit, turn right at a junction and head west back toward the Ward Reservation. Immediately after crossing the property boundary, stay straight at a triangle junction and begin descending. The trail drops through a notably stone-flecked section and then reaches a 5-way intersection (17).

Cross over the wide, red-blazed Old Chestnut Street and bear right on an unmarked singletrack path, following an arrow pointing "to Beth's Trail." Bear right at an unmarked junction. At an intersection (18), cross over the wide Ward Trail and descend to a junction (19) with Margaret's Trail. Turn left and head west. After passing a spur path on the left to a view out across Rubbish Meadow wetland, you reach jct. 20.

Take a right onto Greg's Trail. This is about as close as you can get to a track on trails; it's mostly flat and comparatively rock free, and you can really open it up for long stretches. Staying left at two junctions with bootleg trails leading off property, go 0.9 miles back around to a junction (21) with Margaret's Trail. If pressed for time, skipping Greg's Trail would shave nearly a mile off your run (but doing it twice instead might be a lot more fun).

Turn right and follow Margaret's Trail southwest. Quickly reach an amazing boardwalk bridge over a greenish-tinted cove of the Mars Swamp wetland, looking a bit like a slice of the Everglades transplanted to New England. From there, continue southwest up and over the ledges of a low ridge to a junction (22) with Bay Circuit Trail. Go straight across this 5-way intersection, then follow the red-blazed BCT south, first descending to a low area and then gradually climbing to jct. 23 at a paved road. Turn right and descend back to the trailhead.

Optional Extensions   A short out-and-back excursion on Bog Trail leads to a pretty, water-willow-ringed kettle pond. On the south side of Ward, several trails encircle open fields and offer a pleasant change of pace from the more forested trails.

NEARBY The Andover Village Improvement Society (AVIS) manages numerous conservation properties with runnable trails. Several miles northwest, trail networks at **Indian Ridge**, **Doyle Link Park**, **Baker's Meadow Reservation**, the **Shawsheen River**, and **Vale Reservation** can be linked together via the BCT. Flanking High Plain Road just north of I-495, there are interconnected trail networks at sites like **Wood Hill**, **Bald Hill**, **Rafton Reservation**, and **Fish Brook Reservation**.

Boardwalk bridge along Margaret's Trail at the Ward Reservation in Andover.

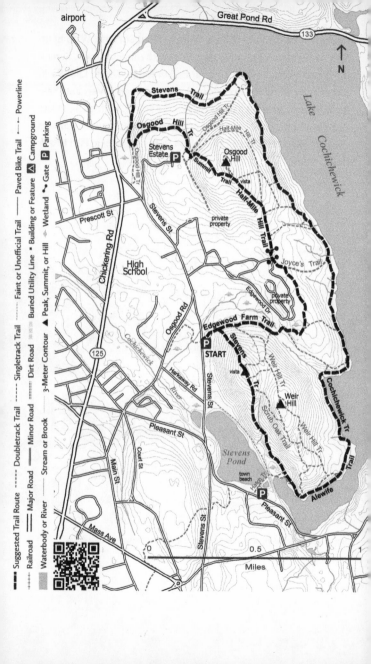

DISTANCE 5.3 Miles **TOWN** North Andover
DIFFICULTY RATING Moderate **TRAIL STYLE** Loop
TRAIL TYPE Singletrack **TOTAL ASCENT** 425 Feet

Weir Hill (pronounced "wire") is a twin-summited hill rising about 300 feet above the western shore of Lake Cochichewick. It is connected via trails to Osgood Hill just to the north and Stevens Pond (with a town beach) just to the south. This route roughly circles the hills, each of which has stunning views of the surrounding landscape, while also climbing over them. The grade varies widely from flat to steep, and the terrain ranges from soft and smooth to rugged and rocky. It is rather rooty in spots and occasionally muddy (some sections may be slick). One stretch briefly traces the outskirt of an assisted living facility; make sure to stay on the trail and respect private property. "You are here" maps are placed at many of the trail junctions, though not all, and there are many unmarked junctions throughout the site. Lake Cochichewick is a town reservoir, and neither swimming nor wading is allowed.

DIRECTIONS   From I-495, exit 100A, take Rte. 114 east for 1 mile. Turn left onto Rte. 133 and go 0.2 miles east. At the lights, go straight onto Andover Street and continue for 0.6 miles. Bear right at the fork and continue for 0.2 miles to an intersection. Go straight for 0.1 miles, turn left onto Stevens Street, and continue for 0.8 miles to parking for the Weir Hill Reservation on the right, marked by a Trustees signpost.
GPS   "Weir Hill Reservation, 65 Stevens Street"

TRAIL   From the trailhead kiosk, follow the main trail up the hill toward the woods. At the first junction, bear right onto the wide, yellow-blazed Stevens Trail and begin climbing southeast at a moderately steep grade. At the open western summit of Weir Hill, there are several stone benches and an expansive west-facing vista. From the top, descend southeast on Stevens Trail to a junction with Hatch Trail at the bottom, passing several marked and unmarked junctions along the way. The trail is wide and the footing is very good.

Continue straight on what is now Alewife Trail, still following yellow-circle blazes. Several unmarked paths diverge to either side; stay on the marked trail. Lake Cochichewick is now to the right. In a few hundred feet, continue straight at a junction where Scrub Oak Trail leads left up the hill. Stay straight at another marked junction where Weir Hill Trail leads left up the hill. In 0.2 miles, the Alewife Trail bears left and quietly becomes Cochichewick Trail, still blazed yellow. Follow this trail north. Although there are some roots, the footing is generally good, and many of the muddy or sensitive areas are crossed with boardwalks.

Stay straight at a junction where the yellow-blazed route changes names again to Edgewood Farm Trail, and there is an old foundation on the right. At a junction marked only by a property boundary sign, stay straight on an unblazed trail (do not follow the yellow-blazed Edgewood Farm Trail that leads left up the hill and back around to the trailhead).

For the next mile or so, trace the western shore of the lake; there are no markings at first. Stay straight, as numerous named and unnamed trails lead left up the hill. Cross several boardwalks, pass a few water-side sitting benches, and traverse some rooty sections. At one point the trail angles partway up the hill before dropping back down to the water's edge. Along this stretch the path becomes the orange-blazed Lake Trail and passes through a grove of large old "legacy" trees. After rounding a point at the northern end of the loop on a short, circular portion of the blue-blazed Osgood Hill Trail, follow the green-blazed Stevens Trail west above a wet area adjacent to the lake. The trail undulates along the base of the hill and then swings south and rises to a junction with Osgood Hill Trail.

Take a sharp left onto the blue-blazed Osgood Hill Trail and climb at a moderate grade, slowly curving right, to a junction just below the Stevens Estate. There is a rapid series of junctions here. Bear left, then right (Osgood Hill Trail goes left), then right again (Half-Mile Hill Trail), and arrive at a junction with Summit Trail (if you reach a sign kiosk, you've gone too far). Take a sharp left on the red-blazed Summit Trail and climb. You'll cross over the top of the hill, pass a short figure-8 side loop around the actual summit of Osgood Hill on the left, and come out of the woods at the upper end of a large grassy field. This is Half-Mile Hill, where several Adirondack chairs look out across the magnificent southeasterly vista.

Adirondack chairs at the vista near the top of Half-Mile Hill Trail in North Andover.

Bearing right, drop down through the open field on a narrow ribbon of dirt singletrack. Near the middle of the hill, join with Half-Mile Hill Trail. Bear right near the bottom and follow the edge of the woods to a closed gate at an assisted living facility. Go around the gate to a paved lane. Go right on the lane for a few feet, and then go left on the wide gravel path across the grass. Follow Joyce's Path as it veers left into the woods, then bear right at an unmarked junction. Staying off the private property to the right, follow the path around the outer edge of a fenced-off garden and then back into the woods. Stay right at a junction and then follow the yellow-blazed Edgewood Farm Trail back to the parking area, staying right at all remaining junctions (except any marked as going off property).

Optional Extension At the end of the route, an excellent mini-loop option is to take the blue-blazed Weir Hill Trail up and over the western summit of Weir Hill to the lakeshore at the bottom on the other side, turn right on Alewife Trail, and then take a final right turn onto the red-blazed Scrub Oak Trail up and over the western summit back to the parking lot. All of the trails are fun to run and often slightly less crowded. This smaller loop totals about 2 miles.

NEARBY   A few miles to the west, you can do a mostly flat 10-mile out-and-back run on the **Merrimack River Trail** along the Merrimack River in Andover, starting from a trailhead off of Old River Road (be *very* wary of poison ivy here). Together, the mostly gentle Dudley Porter Trail and Merrill Trail ring Kenoza Lake at **Winnekenni Park** and **Isaac Merrill Park** in Haverhill, with several alternate branches and scenic offshoot loops possible along the way.

DISTANCE 4.5 Miles   **TOWN** Newburyport
DIFFICULTY RATING Easy   **TRAIL STYLE** Loop
TRAIL TYPE Doubletrack   **TOTAL ASCENT** 245 Feet

With miles of scenic trails tucked into the woods on a bluff above the Merrimack River, Maudslay State Park offers an easily accessible, well-maintained running destination. It is a former estate, with a number of historical buildings and features scattered throughout the park, as well as laurel thickets, gardens, fields, ponds, and wetlands; it's especially attractive during the spring and early-summer months when the abundant flowering plants are in full bloom. This route incorporates parts of both the Healthy Heart and Merrimack River Trails, among others, visiting most parts of the park and providing a good gateway for future exploration.

DIRECTIONS   From I-95, exit 86, go east on Rte. 113 for about half a mile. Turn left on Noble Street (just past the cemetery). Turn left on Ferry Street (which becomes Pine Hill Road and then Curzon Mill Road) and go about 2 miles to the large paved parking area (fee) on your left.

GPS   "88 Curzon Mill Road"

TRAIL   From the parking lot, cross the street and pass through the stone wall. The park headquarters building is on the left. Immediately bear right at the first fork and cross the open field on the narrow dirt track of Pine Trail (not marked at this end). Enter the woods at the north end. Pass Overlook Road and Fire Road Trails on the left and reach an intersection with Main Road near the gate house. Go straight and then curve left on North Road. Gradually descend through the

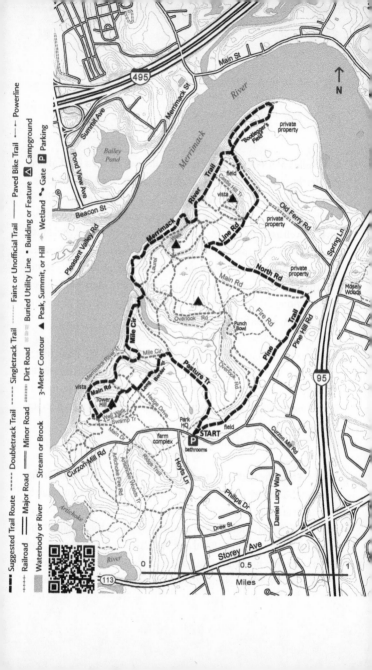

woods to an intersection. Take a sharp right on Line Road and follow it up the hill and around the east side of Castle/Moulton's Hill. Portions of this section are out in the open. At an unmarked junction, go right and descend to a wooded saddle.

Go straight/north for a lollipop loop in the woods to the west of a farm. This area is called Bootlegger's Field. The western part of this loop is right above the bank of the Merrimack River. Back at the saddle, bear right and climb the hill to the junction with Line Road.

Staying straight, follow Castle Hill Trail southwest along the bluff above the river, staying right at all junctions. Take a sharp right on Laurel Walk trail and descend the hill. Bear right again and follow the lower part of this loop, which traces the bank of the river. Several side paths lead right to rocky ledges that are not open to the public.

At a concrete dam, go right and follow the path around the shore of Flowering Pond. Go right on Mile Circle. After passing an unmarked trail on the right, go right on Main Road. Climb gradually, mostly out in the open but also through occasional rhododendron thickets. Stay on Main Road at all junctions. At an intersection near a cottage and covered well, go left and climb over Tower Hill on Well Walk.

On the other side of Tower Hill, go right and pass an old mine. Go right on Hedge Drive briefly, and then go left on Long Border Trail. At the end of a hedge tunnel, descend a steep set of stone steps. Pass through a dense rhododendron thicket and cross two hidden concrete bridges; the trail is briefly very narrow here. Turn right on Mile Circle, then immediately take another right on Pasture Road and follow it back to the trailhead.

NEARBY Right on the other side of I-95, dogs are allowed off-leash at **Moseley Woods**, which features a mile-long loop trail, a playground, and (limited) free parking. Across the river in Amesbury, the north and south sections of **Woodsom Farm** feature a nice, diverse network of trails, some of which run through open fields. The **Salisbury Point Ghost Trail** rail trail in Salisbury makes for an easy, flat, and well-shaded out-and-back run (4 miles total) on packed gravel. On **Plum Island,** the Hellcat Interpretive Trail Marsh Loop is a short, accessible boardwalk path featuring a detour to a salt-pannes observation area; it's a little bit like running on a deck with lots of steps and twists and turns, right in the marsh. Combined with the nearby Dunes loop, you can log a few miles.

DISTANCE 4.5 Miles   **TOWN** Ipswich
DIFFICULTY RATING Moderate   **TRAIL STYLE** Loop
TRAIL TYPE Singletrack/Doubletrack   **TOTAL ASCENT** 190 Feet

Long famous among local trail runners for several annual races, Willowdale State Forest features a tremendous amount of serene, rolling doubletrack and singletrack trail. Most major intersections/ junctions are marked with numbered posts, but some posts are missing. Also, the trails are neither named nor blazed, and flooding can render some low sections impassable, so navigation is a significant challenge here and describing a suggested route is especially hard. This lollipop loop starts and ends from a trailhead on the south side of the property and roughly follows part of the course of one of the races through the center of the forest. Some of the most enjoyable running in the region is along the many mostly unmarked, winding singletrack routes that crisscross and thread through the property; these are well worth exploring, but make sure to allow plenty of time for getting turned around the first time.

DIRECTIONS   From I-95, exit 72, take Endicott Road/Washington Street and go 2 miles to Main Street in Topsfield. Turn left and go 0.3 miles north on Main Street. Take a right onto Ipswich Road and go 2.7 miles to Ipswich Road/Topsfield Road to the parking lot on the left. Parking for Willowdale State Forest is on the north side of the road, and there is a limited amount of roadside parking for Bradley Palmer State Park on the south side of the road.
GPS   "Bradley Palmer Parking, 298 Topsfield Road"

TRAIL   Starting from marker 42 at the parking area, go north up the rise on the wide path, passing singletrack paths on either side along

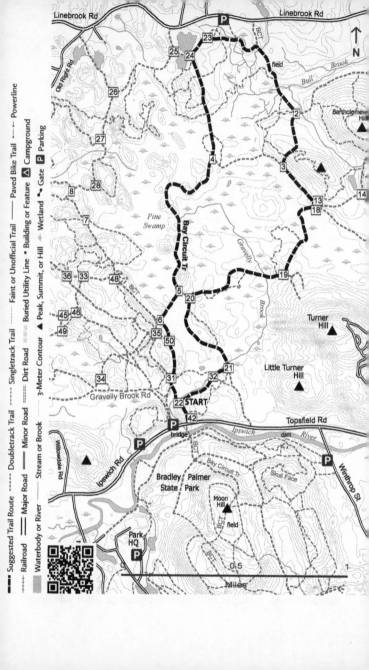

the way. In about 200 yards, bear right at junction 22 and go northeast to an intersection at jct. 32. Go straight through and continue to jct. 21. Turn left and go northwest, passing both ends of a fun singletrack path alternative on the right along the way. At jct. 20, bear right and go east to an open marshy area along Gravelly Brook. On the other side of the wetland crossing, go up a hill to jct. 19 (marked in red on a tree). Bear left and go north to jct. 18, about 2 miles from the start.

At jct. 18, turn left and immediately stay left at jct. 13. Go northwest to jct. 3. Go right and climb the hill to jct. 2, then bear left. Pass a marsh on the left and then rise up into a field (several narrower singletrack paths lead left along the way). Bear left across the field and then head back into the woods. The next section coincides with the Bay Circuit Trail (BCT). Stay straight/left at jct. 23 (the Linebrook Road parking area is just north of here).

Turn left at jct. 24 and go about a mile south to jct. 5, staying straight at all intersections and junctions, including jct. 4, and following BCT markers the whole way. At jct. 5, bear right and go a short distance to jct. 6 (where the BCT goes right). Bear left and go a short distance to jct. 50. Stay straight and go south to jct. 31. Bear slightly left at 31. Cross a concrete bridge, then bear right at jct. 22 and go south back over the rise to the trailhead.

Alternate Route Runners more experienced with Willowdale can string together a complicated and challenging but extremely rewarding 11-mile loop around the forest, starting from the same trailhead, that stays almost entirely on narrow, winding, delightfully runnable singletrack trails.

NEARBY Just south of Willowdale and accessible via a footbridge over the Ipswich River, **Bradley Palmer State Park** offers several good trail-running routes, including a 2-mile loop around Moon and Blueberry Hills that can be lengthened by adding in trails going over both. There's a particularly enjoyable singletrack stretch called

"Skull Face" on the northeast side of Moon Hill. In general, the towns of Ipswich and Hamilton are loaded with short dirt trails—such as those at **Appleton Farms**, **Julia Bird Reservation**, and **Pingree Woodland**—that can be strung together with only minor stretches of paved road. The **Discover Hamilton Trail** is an 8-mile loop that combines trails in Bradley Palmer, Pingree, and Appleton Farms. **Old Town Hill** in Newbury also features a small trail network and has great views. **Bald Hill Reservation** in Boxford and **Georgetown-Rowley State Forest** each have sizable trail networks with mixes of singletrack and doubletrack. Last, loops of the magnificent sandy dune trails at **Crane Beach** can be combined for a great, surprisingly hilly 5- to 6-mile trail run/ankle workout, but the site is extremely popular (especially in summer, for the beach) and has a visitation fee.

DISTANCE 4.4 Miles   **TOWN** Gloucester
DIFFICULTY RATING Moderate   **TRAIL STYLE** Loop
TRAIL TYPE Singletrack/Doubletrack   **TOTAL ASCENT** 350 Feet

Ravenswood Park and adjacent conserved lands support a fun network of crushed-stone carriage roads and meandering hiking paths. The forested landscape is extremely stony, and builders did a great job constructing the trails through such tough terrain. Natural features include swamps, vernal pools, ledges, and occasional glacial erratics. This route strings together three singletrack and doubletrack trails into one big loop that roughly circles the park and visits many of the sights. Parking is limited, so getting an early start is recommended.

DIRECTIONS   From Rte. 128, exit 53, take Rte. 133 southeast for 3 miles to Gloucester. From Gloucester, take Rte. 127 southwest for 2 miles to the park entrance on the right, marked by a Trustees signpost. **GPS**   "Ravenswood Park Main Gate"

TRAIL   Starting at the parking area, follow the wide dirt road (Old Salem Road) north past the gate and up the hill into the woods. At junction (jct.) 1, take a right. Follow the orange-blazed Ledge Trail east past jcts. 3, 5, 6, and 10 up to a ledge with a sweeping overlook of Gloucester Harbor. The red-blazed Boulder Field Trail can be used as an alternative to part of the Ledge Trail, but it misses the overlook. Descend past jcts. 9, 11, 12, and 21 to jct. 22. Turn left and go a few dozen feet on Old Salem Road to jct. 23.

Turn right and follow the blue-blazed Fernwood Lake Trail north in a big arc through the northern part of the park (much of this trail is actually located on City of Gloucester Watershed Lands), following the

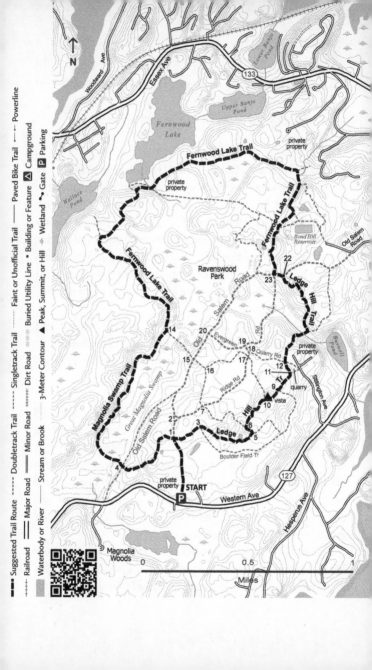

blazes at numerous unmarked junctions. This trail is doubletrack and easy to follow most of the way, though it is frequently quite muddy in spots. In two places at the northern end, side trails on the right lead down to the not especially scenic edge of Fernwood Lake.

At jct. 14, turn right onto the yellow-blazed Magnolia Swamp Trail. This scenic singletrack path undulates through ledgy conifer forest along the western upland edge of Great Magnolia Swamp, home to native sweetbay magnolias, before veering left and traversing the swamp on a long, narrow boardwalk to jct. 4. East of the swamp, the trail rises and falls over a few low knolls as it heads east. At jct. 1, turn right to return to the trailhead.

NEARBY   A quarter mile west on Rte. 127, an out-and-back trail run can be made from the **Magnolia Woods** parking area to **Rafe's Chasm** along the shore (3 miles total). Farther east, Cape Ann offers several excellent trail-running sites in Rockport and Gloucester, including **Dogtown Woods**, **South Woods**, and the **Lanesville** and **Pigeon Cove** quarry lands.

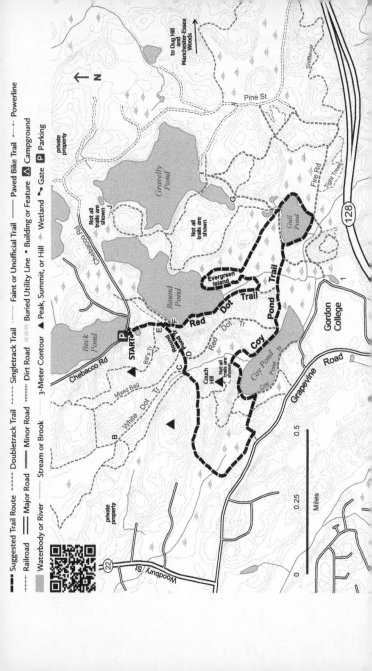

DISTANCE 3.5 Miles **TOWNS** Hamilton, Wenham, and Manchester-by-the-Sea
DIFFICULTY RATING Easy/Moderate **TRAIL STYLE** Loop
TRAIL TYPE Singletrack/Doubletrack/Dirt Road **TOTAL ASCENT** 100 Feet

Chebacco Woods is an amalgamation of town-maintained conservation parcels, jointly owned and managed by Hamilton and
Manchester-by-the-Sea. The southern side abuts the private Gordon
College in Wenham, and the trail networks blend seamlessly. The
main trails are mostly lightly rolling doubletrack paths, but there
are also several wide, flat dirt roads as well as a number of narrow,
twisty, and hilly singletrack trails scattered around the site. The parts
right along the ponds are especially scenic. Signage and blazing
are occasional, but they sometimes don't match what's shown on
available maps.

DIRECTIONS From Rte. 128, exit 47, take Rte. 22 north for 3 miles.
Turn right on Essex Street/Rte. 22 and go 0.3 miles east. Turn right
on Chebacco Road and go 0.6 miles southeast to several small dirt
parking pullouts on the right (Beck Pond is on the left). The entrance
is marked by a white "Chebacco Woods" sign on a wooden post.
GPS "Chebacco Woods, Hamilton"

TRAIL Starting from trailhead, pass a metal gate and follow the wide
dirt path south uphill into the woods. Pass a sign kiosk and small
pool on the right, and then pass an unmarked singletrack trail on the
right at the top of the rise. Just beyond, go right at junction (jct.) E
and follow the white-blazed Round Pond Trail southwest. Pass a
junction with another singletrack path on the right, then stay straight
again at a junction (D) with a red-blazed doubletrack trail (Red Dot

Trail) on the left. Turn left at jct. C, then stay straight at the next two junctions and follow the path for about half a mile around a hill on the left. Go left at a junction south of the hill, then cross an intersection and arrive at the western shore of Coy Pond.

Turn left and trace the shore of the pond on the wide, blue-blazed Coy Pond Trail, staying right at unmarked junctions with singletrack trails on the left. Cross a boardwalk over a marshy cove north of the pond, then stay straight at a junction with a red-blazed trail on the left. Stay right at the next junction, cross another marshy area, and then bear left at a junction and arrive at a beach on the northwest shore of Gull Pond.

Turn right and follow the dirt road along the south shore of Gull Pond. Take a left at an intersection and keep tracing the pond shore. At the next junction, north of the pond, bear right and then immediately left. Follow the straight path across a low area. At a junction, go right and take the Evergreen Island loop trail north to the south shore of Round Pond. Curving left, follow the trail south to a junction. Turn right and cross a few bridges. At a junction, turn right and follow the red-blazed trail north along the western shore of Round Pond. At jct. F, turn left on the wide path and go up and over the rise back to the trailhead.

Optional Extensions   The small hills northwest of Coy Pond, south-west of Gull Pond, northeast of Gull Pond, and east of Round Pond all have trails worth exploring.

NEARBY   Chebacco Woods anchors the western end of an undeveloped area absolutely teeming with great trail networks just north of Rte. 128 on the North Shore. It is complicated but possible to run almost all the way from here to the ocean entirely on the trails of this sweet string of pearls. In the middle, the **Manchester / Essex Woods** complex has excellent interconnected loops in the **Dug Hill / Millstone Hill / Candlewood Hill / Cedar Swamp / Cathedral**

Pines / Agassiz Rock vicinity, all accessible from parking areas right along School Street/Southern Avenue. Just east of that, the **Haskell Pond** area also boasts a dense trail system. And at the eastern end, both the **Tompson Street Reservation** and the **Red Rocks** conservation area in Gloucester have terrific trail networks with frequent seacoast vistas from atop bare granite balds (though the Red Rocks trails are currently less developed). Most of these trails are moderate to challenging due to steep, rocky terrain, or navigation concerns. Just south of Rte. 128, the **Beverly Commons Conservation Area** features a dense, well-maintained system of trails, accessible from a trailhead at the end of Greenwood Avenue.

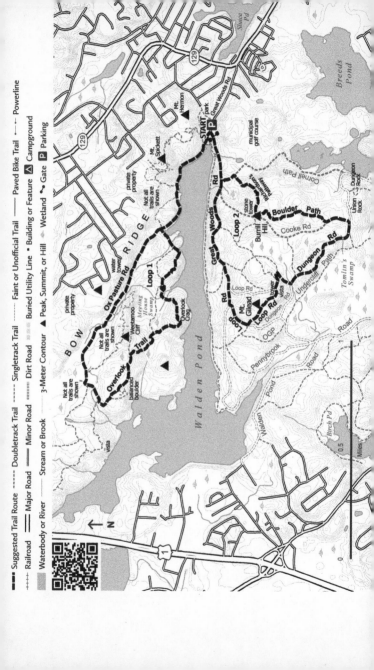

— Suggested Trail Route ----- Doubletrack Trail ----- Singletrack Trail ----- Faint or Unofficial Trail —— Paved Bike Trail - + - Powerline
+++ Railroad —— Major Road ===== Minor Road ==== Dirt Road ▓▓▓ Buried Utility Line ▪ Building or Feature △ Campground P Parking
—— Waterbody or River —— Stream or Brook —— 3-Meter Contour ▲ Peak, Summit, or Hill ✿ Wetland ☙ Gate P Parking

↑ N

B O W

R I D G E

Breeds
Pond

Mt.
Hermon

129

129

START
park

P

Great Woods Rd

Sluce
Pd

municipal
golf course

Cornell Path

private
property

Mt.
Spickett

Not all
trails are
shown

water
tower

Ox Pasture Rd

private
property

Loop 1

Weetamoo
Cliff

Meeting
House
Swamp

Not all
trails are
shown

Overlook
Trail

balanced
boulder

Not all
trails are
shown

vista

Overlook
Ledge

W a l d e n   P o n d

Great
Woods
Rd

Great
Woods
Rd

Loop 2

stone
tower

Burrill
Hill

Boulder   Path

Cooke Rd

Union Rd

Dungeon
Rock

Mt.
Gilead

tower

vista

Loop Rd

Dungeon
Rd

Underscliff
Path

Dungeon
Rd

Loop Rd

OGP

Pennybrook

Tomlin's
Swamp

Loop 2

Walden
Pond

Birch Pd

Road

Road

0   0.5
|————|————|
Miles

DISTANCE 6.3 Miles **TOWN** Lynn
DIFFICULTY RATING Moderate/Challenging **TRAIL STYLE** Loop(s)
TRAIL TYPE Singletrack/Doubletrack/Dirt Road **TOTAL ASCENT** 475 Feet

Lynn Woods is a big municipal forest park—the nation's second largest, actually—located within thirty minutes of downtown Boston. It frames three sizable ponds—Birch, Breeds, and Walden (no, not *that* Walden Pond)—and borders several residential neighborhoods and a golf course. If there's one distinct feature of Lynn Woods, it's glacial erratics; there are so very many boulders dotting the landscape here, from person size to house size. Smooth granite ledges are also plentiful throughout. The property is laced with a dense network of trails and old fire roads, more than 30 miles in total. North of Walden Pond, trails visit Weetamoo Cliff, Mt. Spickett, Mt. Hermon, and several scenic overlooks. There are numerous unblazed trails in this section, some of which are very technical and challenging. South of Walden Pond, the Great Woods Path, Birch Pond Trail, and other routes trace the shore path of the pond, climb to the Stone Tower on Burrill Hill, visit the Dungeon Rock cave, and explore numerous cliffs, ledges, and other natural features, and there's at least one sweeping scenic vista of the city skyline to the south. This suggested route combines both halves of the forest and passes many of the worthwhile sights.

DIRECTIONS From I-95, exit 63B, take Rte. 129 east. Go around the rotary and follow Rte. 129 east for 2.1 miles. Turn right on Great Woods Road and go 0.3 miles to the spacious parking area by the ball field at the end.
GPS "Lynn Woods Reservation Parking Lot, 118 Great Woods Road"

TRAIL   *Loop 1: North of Walden Pond*   Starting at the parking area, pass through the metal gate and follow the dirt path up toward the right side of the dam. Take the wide orange-blazed dirt road (Ox Pasture Road) west along the north shore of the pond, staying straight where several blazed and unblazed trails lead up to the right. These trails, which climb and wind around the ledges of Mt. Hermon and Mt. Spickett, are confusingly marked but well worth exploring later. At 0.5 miles, stay straight at a junction with Overlook Trail on the left. Follow Ox Pasture Road northwest through a valley below the southern slope of Bow Ridge for almost a mile to another junction with Overlook (passing an unmarked junction with a fun but hard to follow path called Wicked Hard Trail on the left).

> *Optional Extension*   To add an extra mile or so, continue north from this junction on the Deep Woods Trail, then take lefts onto Beaver Trail and Shark's Tooth East trails and follow them back around to Overlook Trail. These trails are unmarked and may be challenging to navigate.

Turn left onto the red-blazed Overlook Trail and follow it all the way back to the lower junction with Ox Pasture Road. Along the way, take the time to visit the various spurs out to scenic overlooks above the pond, Balanced Boulder, Weetamoo Cliff, Great Frog Boulder, and Overlook Crag. Many trails, including Meeting House Swamp, make excellent alternate routes. Take Ox Pasture Road back to the Great Woods parking area.

Loop 2: South of Walden Pond   Start the second loop by heading up the Great Woods Path. Take the first left on Cornell Trail, then turn right and climb Richardson Pathway to the Stone Tower on Burrill Hill. Take Boulder Path down past more glacial erratics to Cooke Road, then go left to Dungeon Road. Here, a short out-and-back run to the left will bring you to Union Rock and Dungeon Rock. Go right on Dungeon Road for a half mile, then take the second right.

Climb to the first junction, then turn left and climb to the steel tower on top of Mt. Gilead. There's a terrific view of Boston from a nearby south-facing ledge. Bearing left, descend Loop Road to Dungeon Road. Turn right and descend to Great Woods Road. Take a right and descend back to the parking area.

Other trails in the southern section trace the shores of ponds, summit Mt. Moriah and Cedar Hill, and pass by more huge rocks. Some more worth exploring include Undercliff Path, Star Wars Trail, Bow Ridge Trail, Han Solo, and Birch Pond Trail.

NEARBY Just to the west, Saugus's **Breakheart Reservation** features a large network of trails around seven rocky hills; a great loop can be made combining the Ridge and Saugus River Trails, and the Eagle Hill, Fox Run, and Silver Lake Trails are nice, too. Just to the east, there is a 3- to 4-mile lollipop-loop option on trails east of **Spring Pond** in Peabody. A 3- to 4-mile loop can be made at **Salem Woods / Forest River Conservation Area** in Salem, and weekly trail races are held there in summer.

Walden Pond from Overlook Crag at Lynn Woods.

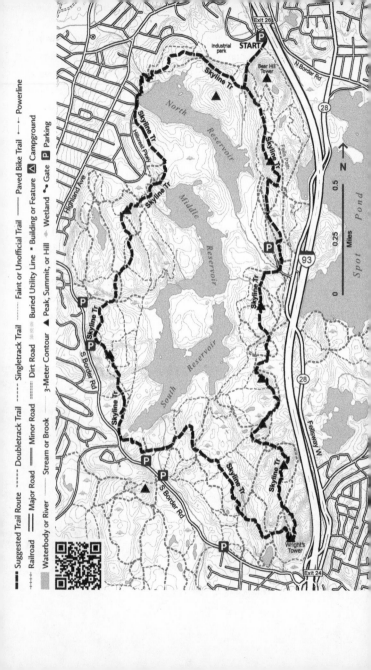

■ Suggested Trail Route ++++ Railroad ------ Waterbody or River ----- Doubletrack Trail ═══ Major Road ──── Stream or Brook ······ Singletrack Trail ░░░ Minor Road ----- Faint or Unofficial Trail ▒▒▒ Dirt Road ─── Paved Bike Trail --- Powerline ──── 3-Meter Contour — Buried Utility Line ▲ Peak, Summit, or Hill • Building or Feature ᚐ Wetland ⛣ Gate ⬜ P Parking △ Campground

N

Exit 26
START ⬜ P
Industrial park
Bear Hill Tower ▲
N Border Rd

Skyline Tr

North Reservoir

▲

Fells Path

28

Skyline Tr

Hillcrest Pkwy

Skyline Tr

Middle Reservoir

Highland Ave

Spot Pond

0   0.25   0.5
Miles

Skyline Tr

⬜ P

93

Skyline Tr

⬜ P

South Reservoir

Skyline Tr
S Border Rd
⬜ P
⬜ P

28

Fellsway W

Skyline Tr

▲
S Border Rd
⬜ P
⬜ P

Skyline Tr

Skyline Tr

⬜ P

Wright's Tower

Exit 24

DISTANCE 8 Miles **TOWNS** Stoneham, Medford, and Winchester
DIFFICULTY RATING Challenging **TRAIL STYLE** Loop
TRAIL TYPE Singletrack/Doubletrack **TOTAL ASCENT** 935 Feet

Due to its proximity to the city and extensive network of trails, the Middlesex Fells Reservation may be the premier trail-running destination just north of Boston. It's actually several sites in one, and there are numerous great loop options here. This difficult route in the western half follows the rugged, rocky, and rooty course of the white-blazed Skyline Trail, which, as the name implies, heads for the highlands whenever there's any kind of hill to go over and hits many of the scenic vistas. The oval-shaped route's elevation profile constantly rises and falls, and there are many worthwhile side excursions to take along the way. Other named loops at the western half of the Fells include Mountain Bike Loop, Reservoir Trail, and Long Pond Nature Trail; all are good for running and have scenic draws of their own, though they are more variable in terms of surface and include more rough dirt-road sections. The orange-blazed Reservoir Loop offers a slightly easier and shorter (5.2-mile) alternative mostly inside the Skyline Trail loop. There are numerous small parking areas around the perimeter of the reservation. Note that access to the reservoirs themselves is restricted. Also, beware that unleashed dogs have sometimes been a problem for runners here in the past.

DIRECTIONS From I-93, exit 26, look for the small paved parking lot on the south side of Fallon Road, near a green metal gate to the left of a building-supply company fence.
GPS "Bear Hill Parking Lot, Stoneham"

TRAIL   Starting at the parking area, follow the flat, wide dirt path of Dike Road south into the woods. Pass an unmarked junction on the left and intersection C1–6. In 0.3 miles, at intersection C2–1, turn left onto the Skyline Trail. Follow the rugged singletrack trail up the hill for 0.2 miles to junction C2–2 at Bear Hill Trail.

> *Optional Extension*   For the first of many possible short side excursions, go left at junction C2–2 and follow Bear Hill Trail northeast up the slope to Bear Hill Road, then turn left and climb to Bear Hill Tower at the top of the hill. Return the way you came. In total, this extension adds 0.3 miles to your run.

From Bear Hill Trail, continue south on Skyline Trail, carefully following the markers at every junction and intersection. The trail climbs over the top of Winthrop Hill, drops down the other side, and then winds back and forth over low ridges and past several wetlands. After passing a parking area near Sheepfold, the trail climbs over numerous low ridges and rocky knolls, including Gerry Hill, Silver Mine Hill, Wenepoykin Hill, and Little Pine Hill.

At just over 3 miles, the Skyline Trail reaches Wright's Tower at the summit of Pine Hill, where there is a sweeping view of the Boston city skyline to the south. Bear right at the tower and descend the hill via steep switchbacks. At the bottom, go northwest and negotiate another series of low hills and ridges as you head toward the southern end of South Reservoir. Several roads lead south to alternate parking areas at the south side of the reservation in this section. At 4.5 miles, you'll pass very close to several parking areas along South Border Road, and then briefly parallel the road itself.

From South Border Road, go north over more hills and ridges, including one significantly larger one. After crossing Molly's Spring Road (and briefly following it east), climb north up and over Nanepashemet Hill. On the other side, the trail roller-coasters up and down numerous other low hills and ridges.

Optional Extension At Molly's Spring Road, turn left instead of right and go 0.1 miles west toward the Long Pond Parking Area. At a junction, follow the Cranberry Pool Path / Long Pond Nature Trail north. This series of three yellow-blazed loops adds about 1.5 miles total.

At 6.7 miles, you'll reach a junction with the Wyman Path at the west end of North Reservoir. Follow markers around the edge, then reenter the woods at the northern end of the pavement. After dipping down to a low area, the trail swings east and climbs over several high points on Money Hill. After crossing over the combined Reservoir Trail and Mountain Bike Loop, the Skyline Trail climbs over one last hill before descending back down to Dike Road at C2–1. Turn left here and return back to the parking area 0.3 miles to the north.

NEARBY On the other side of I-93, the eastern part of **Middlesex Fells** features another dense network of paths, including marked ones like the 5.2-mile (one-way) Cross Fells Trail (blue blazes), the very hilly 3.7-mile Rock Circuit Trail loop (white blazes), and the 1.4-mile Crystal Spring Trail (red blazes). There are several parking areas, and unmarked trail entrances near Pinnacle Rock off Brazil Street and East Border Road in Malden are easily accessible from the Orange Line's Oak Grove Station. A few miles west, there are small networks of wooded trails west of the paved path at **Horn Pond** and at **Horn Pond Mountain / Mt. Towanda** in Woburn.

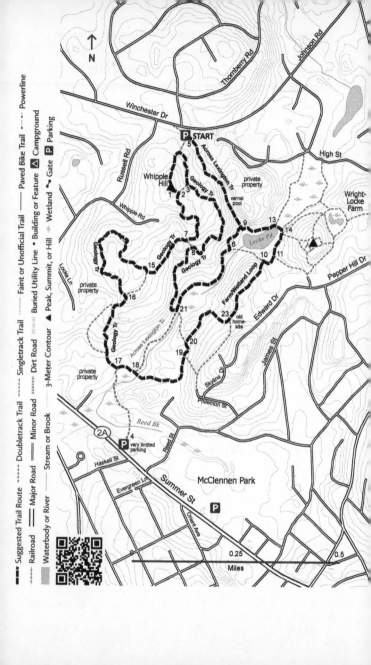

DISTANCE 3 Miles **TOWNS** Lexington and Winchester
DIFFICULTY RATING Easy/Moderate **TRAIL STYLE** Loop(s)
TRAIL TYPE Singletrack/Doubletrack **TOTAL ASCENT** 270 Feet

Whipple Hill is the second-largest conservation area in Lexington. On the northeast side, it borders the Locke Farm and Wright-Locke Farm conservation properties in Winchester, and together all three share a dense, interconnected network of mostly marked and color-coded trails with numerous numbered junctions. This suggested route combines a mix of the red, green, and yellow loop paths and features a fair amount of elevation change throughout. Locke Pond, a community farm (with a seasonal farm stand), the seasonal stream corridor of Whipple Brook, and the bare-rock summit of 375-foot Whipple Hill (the highest point in Lexington) are the most notable natural features at the site, though there are also boulders, stone walls, rock piles, rock outcrops, wildflowers, old foundations, a rusted vehicle hulk, and several vernal pools scattered throughout the woods. Dogs are allowed off-leash.

DIRECTIONS From I-95, exit 50B, take Middlesex Turnpike south for 0.4 miles to where it becomes Lowell Street. Stay straight and follow Lowell Street southeast for 2 miles. Turn left onto Winchester Drive. Go 0.7 miles on Winchester Drive/Johnson Road. The small parking lot on the right (just past Russell Drive) is marked with a brown wooden sign. Alternate parking can be found at a very small lot on the south side, at Wright-Locke Farm at 82 Ridge Street in Winchester, and a quarter mile to the southeast at McClennen Park in Arlington.

GPS "196 Johnson Road" (alternate: "McClennen Park, Arlington")

TRAIL   From the northern trailhead, follow the blue-blazed Across Lexington Trail southeast for 0.25 miles to a junction (#9), passing a large vernal pool on the left along the way. Turn left and follow the yellow-blazed Farm/Wetland Loop trail east, north of Locke Pond. In a few hundred feet, stay right at jct. 13, then continue east a short distance to jct. 14.

> *Optional Extension*   Turn left and follow the narrow trail along the west shore of a wetland for 0.15 miles to a trailhead along High Street. Watching for traffic, turn right and follow High Street around the corner. In a few hundred feet, just before a driveway, turn right at an easy-to-miss trailhead and follow the trail south along the east side of the wetland to a junction. Turn left and go a few hundred feet to a junction. Bear left and follow the trail as it curves to the right around the western edge of a field at Wright-Locke Farm. In 0.1 miles, bear left at a junction, then go another 0.1 miles to a junction with the green-blazed Conservation Trail. Turn right and climb a low hill. At a rapid series of junctions, bear right, left, right, and straight. After dropping down the west side of the hill, you'll arrive back at Locke Pond (at jct. 14).

From the northeast side of Locke Pond, go southwest on the yellow-blazed Farm/Wetland Loop trail for 0.6 miles, staying on it at numerous junctions along the way (11, 10, 23, 20, 19, and several unmarked ones). At jct. 18, go left on the combined blue-blazed Across Lexington Trail and red-blazed Geology Loop trail.

Bear right at jct. 17 and begin following the red arrow markers up the hill. The trail winds around the hillside and passes several numbered junctions; stay on the red trail. At a large boulder, bear left and pass right below the rock and then climb to jct. 2 just below the top. Turn left and cross over the summit. On a clear day, you can see Mt. Wachusett and Mt. Monadnock from the top. Then begin descending the north side. At an unmarked junction just before the bottom, bear right and follow the red arrows across the east side of the hill, staying on the marked trail at several junctions, and down to the bottom. At jct. 21, turn left and follow the blue-blazed Across Lexington Trail back to the parking lot.

NEARBY **Arlington's Great Meadows** conservation area (which is actually in Lexington) features several miles of trails, and a not entirely connected string of relatively urban trails (some paved) flanks the banks of the **Mystic River** and **Alewife Brook** a few miles to the east in Arlington, Medford, and Winchester.

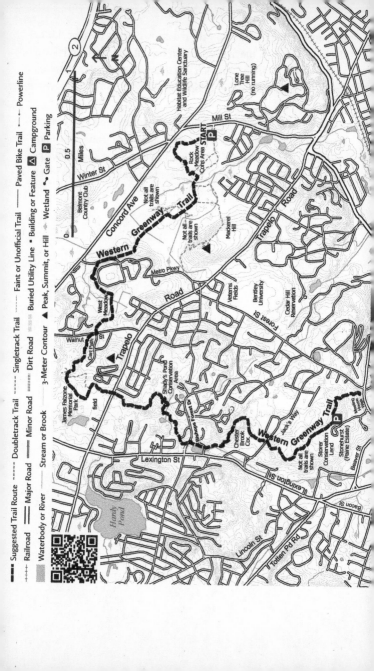

Suggested Trail Route ----- **Doubletrack Trail** ------ **Singletrack Trail** ----- **Faint or Unofficial Trail** ------ **Paved Bike Trail** ----- **Powerline**
+++++ **Railroad** ===== **Major Road** ===== **Minor Road** ------ **Dirt Road** ······ **Buried Utility Line** ■ **Building or Feature** ▲ **Campground**
----- **Waterbody or River** ------ **Stream or Brook** ------ **3-Meter Contour** ▲ **Peak, Summit, or Hill** ◦ **Wetland** ✎ **Gate** 🅿 **Parking**

DISTANCE 11 Miles **TOWNS** Belmont and Waltham
DIFFICULTY RATING Easy/Moderate **TRAIL STYLE** Out-and-back
TRAIL TYPE Singletrack/Doubletrack **TOTAL ASCENT** 360 Feet

The Western Greenway (WG) refers to a corridor of undeveloped green spaces in several towns just west of Boston as well as a trail that runs through and connects them. The well-marked 5.5-mile point-to-point trail becomes an 11-mile out-and-back run. This suggested route starts at Rock Meadow Conservation Area in Belmont, but it can easily be done in either direction or in shorter sections. The Western Greenway trail technically also continues east into the Lone Tree Hill trails and Mass Audubon's Habitat Sanctuary walking-trail networks.

DIRECTIONS From Rte. 2, exit 131, take Winter Street south 0.1 miles to Concord Avenue. Turn left and then immediately bear right onto Mill Street. Go 0.2 miles south up the hill and then turn right into the driveway for the Rock Meadow Conservation Area, marked with a brown wooden sign. The Rock Meadow parking lot is fairly small. **GPS** "Rock Meadow Conservation Area, 319 Mill Street"

TRAIL Starting at the Rock Meadow trailhead, follow the green leaf markers of the Western Greenway Trail north across open fields, passing the Belmont Victory Gardens on the left. Numerous trails thread through the meadows here, so begin looking for and only following the WG markers. The other trails are nice, though, and can be explored on the way back or afterward. After curving around the meadows and crossing several boardwalks, cross a bridge over Beaver Brook and continue into the Beaver Brook North conservation area. A dense network of paths, trails, and carriage trails crisscross the WG

Trail here. After navigating this warren, arrive at DCR's Metropolitan Parkway road.

Briefly go right on the sidewalk, then reenter the woods and continue west. The WG Trail becomes a singletrack path as it circles through the woods around an apartment complex, crosses West Meadow on boardwalks, and then climbs to a junction with Walnut Street. Cross the street, then go right on the sidewalk to where the trail reenters the woods just north of Cart Path Lane. Follow the narrow trail along the hillside; the vegetation is dense here, and you may even need to duck in a few places. Descend the hill to a soccer field, then bear left and go around the park until you reach Trapelo Road.

Cross Trapelo and begin heading south through Shady Pond Conservation Area and Chester Brook corridor. There are very few side trails in this area, and it's one of the nicest sections of the entire route for running. The WG Trail winds around the forested hillsides and crosses streams on well-built bridges and boardwalks. After crossing Bishops Forest Road, pass below a YMCA camp, pass between two schools, and arrive at Jack's Way road.

Cross the road and continue south into the Chester Brook Woods and Storer Conservation Lands. The marked trail turns to doubletrack and zigzags through a complex system of trails. At the parking lot for Stonehurst (the Robert Treat Paine estate), go left and reenter the woods at a sign pointing to Beaver Street. Follow the WG along Hobbs Trail and Lyman Trail down to its end at Meeting House Walk. Reverse course back to Rock Meadow or choose one of the alternate return routes below.

Alternate Routes   Several alternate route options are possible on either leg of this out-and-back run, most notably in the Stonehurst Estate, Shady's Pond, Mackerel Hill, Beaver Brook North, and Rock Meadow vicinities. There's a particularly nice switchback trail on the north side of Mackerel Hill.

NEARBY A few miles west, there is a moderately difficult, heavily trafficked 3-mile loop on trails and old roads at **Prospect Hill Park** in Waltham. This small site borders I-95, but there are nice views from Boston Rock; access from a parking lot along Totten Pond Road at the north end. To the southeast, across the Charles River and right in the heart of Boston, the **Emerald Necklace** paths along the **Fenway** and **Back Bay Fens**, around **Jamaica Pond**, and in **Olmsted Park**, **Allandale Woods**, **Arnold Arboretum**, and **Franklin Park** provide miles of admittedly urban but still delightful trail running. A few miles south, the **Webster Conservation Area** near Hammond Pond in Newton offers several miles of surprisingly rugged trails; it even has some cliffs!

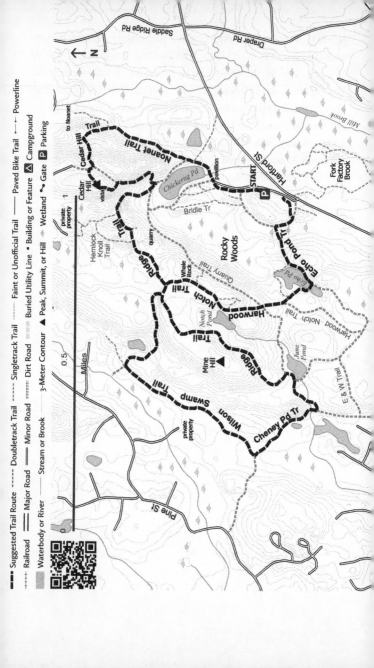

Legend:

■ Suggested Trail Route
┼┼┼┼ Railroad
─── Waterbody or River

- - - - Doubletrack Trail
── Major Road
─── Stream or Brook

- - - - Singletrack Trail
═══ Minor Road
─── 3-Meter Contour

---- Faint or Unofficial Trail
═══ Dirt Road
░░░ Buried Utility Line

── Paved Bike Trail
── Powerline
• Building or Feature ▲ Campground

▲ Peak, Summit, or Hill ⟿ Wetland ⟿ Gate 🅿 Parking

N ←

Saddle Ridge Rd
Draper Rd

to Noanet

Cedar Hill Trail
Noanet Trail
Cedar Hill vista
Chickering Pd
Bridle Tr
Hemlock Knoll Trail
Ridge Trail
quarry
Whale Rock
Notch Trail
Notch Pond
Rocky Woods
Quarry Trail
Harwood Trail
Harwood Notch Trail
Echo Pond Tr
Echo Pd
June Pond
E & W Trail
Ridge Trail
Mine Hill ▲
Wilson Swamp Trail
Cheney Pd Tr
private property
Pine St
pavilion
START
🅿
Hartford St
Mill Brook
Fork Factory Brook

private property 1

0.5
Miles

DISTANCE 4.2 Miles   **TOWN** Medfield

DIFFICULTY RATING Easy/Moderate   **TRAIL STYLE** Figure-8 Loop

TRAIL TYPE Doubletrack   **TOTAL ASCENT** 465 Feet

The Trustees' Rocky Woods reservation features a superbly maintained network of carriage-trail-style dirt roads and wide doubletrack
hiking paths that make for extremely pleasant running, especially
in the more remote parts. Color-coded loops are clearly marked,
most named trails are signed, and there are maps at all numbered
junctions. This route strings together pieces of the various loops for
a good sampling of everything. There are clearly designated leash
and off-leash zones for dogs.

DIRECTIONS From I-95/Rte. 128, exit 31B, take Rte. 109 west for 5.7
miles. Turn right on Hartford Street and go 0.6 miles to the entrance
and large parking lot on the left, marked by a Trustees sign.
GPS "Rocky Woods Reservation Entrance"

TRAIL Starting at the parking area, follow the red-blazed trail north
just left of the paved road to the visitor center, restrooms, and picnic
area by Chickering Pond. At the pond, bear right and cross the outlet
stream. At junction (jct.) 3, take a right on Noanet Trail. Pass a junction
with a connector trail to Powisset Farm on the right. Bear left onto Cedar
Hill Trail and climb at a moderate grade to a junction with Tower Trail.
Go right and then left at unmarked junctions. Cross over the 435-foot
summit of Cedar Hill, and then descend slightly to a south-facing vista
ledge. Drop down to Tower Trail and follow it down to jct. 4.

Turn right and follow the yellow-blazed Ridge Trail north up the
hill. Pass junctions with both ends of Hemlock Knoll Trail (a rocky

quarter-mile horseshoe-shaped partial loop) on the right, then a spur path to an obstructed vista on the left. At jct. 7, turn right on the blue-blazed Wilson Swamp Trail. Stay right at jct. 8, and then descend to jct. 9. Turn left and follow a wide, gently rolling stretch southwest to jct. 10. Go left on Cheney Pond Trail to jct. 13. Go left on Ridge Trail to jct. 12 and then left again around the shore of June Pond to nearby jct. 11.

Take a left and climb at a gentle grade on Ridge Trail to jct. 8. Turn right and then immediately go right again at jct. 7. Follow the yellow-blazed Harwood Notch Trail south along the ridge past Whale Rock on the left. Pass a spur path to a (not-very-impressive) vista on the left, then pass a pond on the right, and then descend to jct. 6.

Go straight across the intersection and follow the yellow-blazed trail down to Echo Pond, passing junctions on the right and left. Cross the footbridge over the pond, then turn left and follow the yellow-blazed trail north to jct. 1. Go right to return to the parking area.

> *Optional Extension*   To add an easy-moderate extra mile, cross Hartford Street to Fork Factory Brook Reservation and follow the orange-blazed lollipop trail loop through fields and woods, around the edges of a big wetland, and past old foundations.

NEARBY   A few miles south, the extensive trail network at **Adams Farm** in Norwood/Walpole offers a little bit of everything, including wide carriage-trail-style dirt roads, cross-country paths through fields, standard hiking trails, and smooth, narrow, winding singletrack routes around low, wooded hills. To the southwest, color-coded trail loops at Medfield's **Noon Hill Reservation** and adjacent **Shattuck Reservation** can be combined for a pleasant run of 10 miles or more. To the west, **Rocky Narrows Reservation** (a.k.a. the Gates of the Charles) in Sherborn has a network of relatively short but scenic trail loops. **Sherborn Town Forest** is another good site to the west, and **Pegan Hill** in Natick also features a few miles of scenic trail.

DISTANCE 3.5 Miles   **TOWN** Dover
DIFFICULTY RATING Moderate   **TRAIL STYLE** Loop
TRAIL TYPE Doubletrack/Singletrack   **TOTAL ASCENT** 275 Feet

The forested Noanet reservation sits as a sprawling sea of green amid dense metro-Boston residential areas. It features views of the distant city skyline from 387-foot Noanet Peak, numerous old mill ponds and wetlands along Noanet Brook, and tons of trails. Together with the adjacent Hale Reservation to the east, the site offers numerous trail loop options on a wide variety of trail types of all difficulty levels. The main parking lot can fill up fast when the weather is nice, so plan your visit accordingly (try early in the morning or late afternoon).

DIRECTIONS From I-95/Rte. 128, exit 31B, take Rte. 109 west. In just under a mile, take a right on Dover Road/Powisset Street and go 2.3 miles to the reservation entrance and dirt parking lot on the right, marked by a Trustees sign. Parking at Noanet is limited to thirty vehicles; street parking is prohibited. Alternate parking may be found at nearby Powisset Farm to the south, adjacent Caryl Park to the north, and adjacent Hale Reservation to the east.

GPS "Noanet Woodlands Parking Lot, 61 Powisset Street"

TRAIL Starting at the main parking area, follow the blue-blazed trail north to junction (jct.) 25. First go left on the wide trail, and then go right at a junction. Bear left at a Y, then left onto the blue-blazed Peabody Loop Trail at jct. 19. Most of this first section is flat to gently rolling.

At jct. 18, turn left and begin following the orange-blazed Larabee Loop Trail clockwise. Stay on this undulating, mostly doubletrack

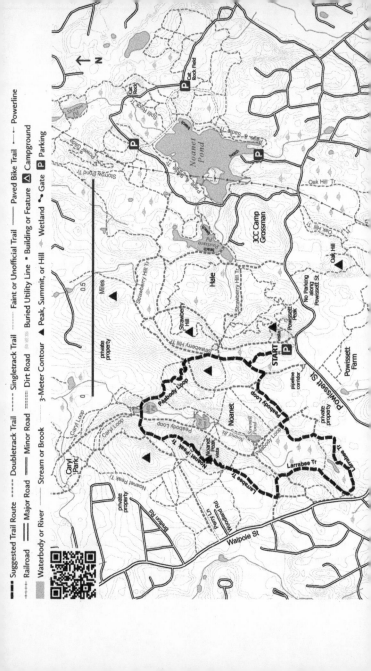

Legend:

- ■■■ Suggested Trail Route
- ┼┼┼ Railroad
- ─── Waterbody or River
- ----- Doubletrack Trail
- ═══ Major Road
- ─── Stream or Brook
- ----- Singletrack Trail
- ─── Minor Road
- ······ Faint or Unofficial Trail
- ╍╍╍ Dirt Road
- ----- Paved Bike Trail
- ~~~~ Buried Utility Line
- ─··─ 3-Meter Contour
- ┼─┼ Powerline
- • Building or Feature
- ▲ Peak, Summit, or Hill
- △ Campground
- ～ Wetland
- P Parking
- ⚲ Gate

N ←

Noanet Pond

Caryl Park

Noanet

Hale

Strawberry Hill

START

Powissett Farm

Walpole St

POWISSETT ST

Brown Rd

Peabody Loop

Caryl Loop

Larrabee Tr

Noanet Peak Tr

JCC Camp Grossman

Cat Rock Field

Oak Hill

trail at all marked and unmarked junctions to jct. 9 (along the way there are several unmarked singletrack trails on the right that are great for running).

At jct. 9, take the rugged, yellow-blazed Noanet Peak Trail north up the steep slope to the open ledge at the top of 387-foot Noanet Peak where there is a sweeping east-facing vista. Continue north and descend the Noanet Peak Trail, passing junctions 47 and 48, to jct. 36 just above the mill site.

Cross the causeway/dam between Upper and Lower Mill Ponds. Then, bearing right, start following the blue-blazed Peabody Loop Trail south at jct. 27. Pass jct. 26 and unmarked junctions with trails on the right and left, then go left at jct. 24. Climb the slope to the east at a moderate grade via switchbacks to a 5-way intersection just past a stone wall. Bear right and head southeast on the wide path to jct. 31. Bear right and head south to intersection 23. From there, go south to jct. 25, then turn left and follow the blue-blazed access trail back to the trailhead.

Optional Extension   For a challenging 2.5-mile loop, go east on the fire lane at intersection 23 toward Hale Reservation. Just below a big ledge, take a left onto a narrow singletrack path at the first unmarked junction. This circuitous trail climbs the ledge and then winds north up and over 374-foot Strawberry Hill. Bearing north and then east, descend the hill and cross an intersection. At a junction, go right and follow the yellow-blazed Strawberry Hill Trail southeast down to a junction just above Powissett Pond. Go right and follow Strawberry Hill Trail south to jct. 9 and take another right. At the top of the rise, bear left onto a narrow, unmarked singletrack path. Follow this difficult path southwest. Stay straight at an unmarked intersection and climb up and over a subsidiary summit of Powissett Peak ("Powissett Patio"). At a junction, go right and then immediately left to climb to the open ledge at the top of 367-foot Powissett Peak where there is a west-facing vista (and a lot of graffiti). Descend the unmarked trail north off the peak. Go right at the first junction, then left at the next. Follow the winding singletrack northwest down the slope to a junction. Bear left and descend to a junction with the yellow-blazed trail. Go left to return to intersection 23.

NEARBY   The large **Hale Reservation** in Dover/Westwood borders Noanet to the east and features a complicated network of roads and trails of all types that surround several ponds and pass by numerous camps, cabins, and beaches. The optional extension described above is just a sampling of Hale's many good options (the "Power Glide" singletrack section is especially fun). The reservation continues south of Dover Road as well. Just south of Noanet is **Powisset Farm**, which has an easy 1.5-mile lollipop-loop trail around meadows and hayfields, the backside of which connects to the southern trails of the Hale Reservation (via Ox Hill Trail). Despite some parking challenges and proximity to the highway, **Cutler Park** in Needham offers miles of trails around Kendrick Pond and the Charles River; the Blue Heron Trail in particular can be used for a mid-distance run. Also adjacent to the highway about 2 miles northeast of Hale is DCR's **Wilson Mountain Reservation** in Dedham; this site features a nice network of trails with a hilly 1.5-mile loop that can be run in either direction. Lastly, Needham Town Forest features a tight maze of mostly unmarked trails; there is limited parking at Horsford Ponds and Farley Pond.

DISTANCE 15 Miles   **TOWNS** Canton, Milton, and Quincy
DIFFICULTY RATING Challenging   **TRAIL STYLE** Out-and-Back
TRAIL TYPE Singletrack
TOTAL ASCENT 1,670 Feet (one-way; North Branch option)

The Blue Hills State Reservation covers a large wooded area just south of Boston and consists of an east–west range of relatively low but imposing hills. It includes many rugged peaks, some with impressive views. This is where many locals go to get their "vert." The steep and rugged Skyline Trail traverses the range, starting about a half mile west of Little Blue Hill on the west side and ending at Shea Rink near Rattlesnake Hill at the east end. In between it visits the summits of Great Blue Hill, Chickatawbut Hill, and numerous other high points. There are two branches of the Skyline Trail in the western part of the reservation; the Skyline Loop Trail combines the north and south branches for a challenging 2.6-mile circuit. There are several other marked loop options at Blue Hills. Yellow-dot loops are short and easy, green-dot loops are moderately challenging, and red-dot loops are challenging. White triangles mark the moderately difficult 6-mile Forest Path Loop in the center of the reservation, while yellow triangles mark the challenging Breakneck Ledge Loop in the western part. Major intersections are marked with 4-digit numbers. In addition to the many rugged singletrack trails, there are also many wide dirt paths with smoother surfaces, particularly in the eastern and southern parts, and the ski slopes of Great Blue Hill are great for running (when there's no snow on them).

DIRECTIONS   From I-93, exit 2, take Rte. 138 north for 0.5 mile to the spacious paved park-and-ride lot on the left. If this lot is full,

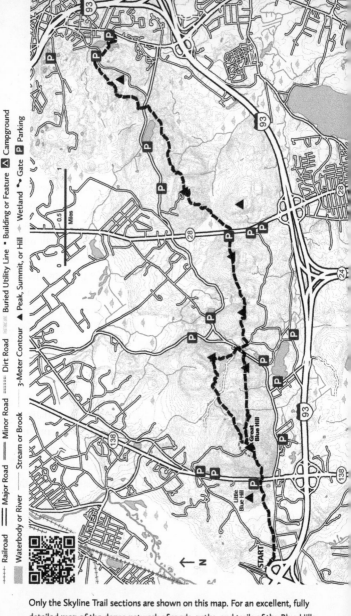

Only the Skyline Trail sections are shown on this map. For an excellent, fully detailed map of the dense network of roads, paths, and trails of the Blue Hills, see DCR's Blue Hills Reservation website.

▬ Suggested Trail Route ----- Doubletrack Trail ----- Singletrack Trail ······ Faint or Unofficial Trail ----- Powerline
┼┼┼┼ Railroad ══ Major Road ══ Minor Road ⠿⠿ Dirt Road ░░░ Buried Utility Line ▪ Building or Feature ▲ Campground
─── Waterbody or River ─── Stream or Brook ── 3-Meter Contour ▲ Peak, Summit, or Hill ⟿ Wetland ⟜ Gate P Parking

0.5 Miles

← N

START

Great Blue Hill

Little Blue Hill

there are other parking areas located near the base of the William F. Rogers ski area about 0.5 miles north and at several locations along Hillside Street and Chickatawbut Road to the east.

GPS "2995 Washington Street, Canton"

TRAIL Starting at the south side of the park-and-ride, take a short link trail south to the Skyline Trail. Turn right and follow the blue blazes about a mile west to the start.

Beginning at a paved stretch of old roadway just north of I-93, exit 1, head east. After crossing over Green Street, Cosmos Path, and K Path, all on relatively flat terrain, climb up and over the lower part of the southern ridge of Little Blue Hill. Pass south of the park-and-ride and reach Washington Street. Cross with great care.

Climb steeply up the west slope of Great Blue Hill. After circling just south of the actual summit, the trail splits into north and south branches. The more challenging North Branch (1.4 miles) descends to a gap, then crosses over Wildcat, Hemenway, and Hancock Hills before descending to Reservation Headquarters near Hillside Street where it rejoins the South Branch. The slightly easier South Branch (1.1 miles) climbs up and over Houghton Hill on its way east to Hillside Street.

From Hillside Street, follow a wide unpaved road a short distance east, then bear left and begin a traverse of the middle section. The trail climbs up and over Tucker Hill, North Boyce Hill, and Buck Hill before dropping down to a parking area along Rte. 28.

From Randolph Avenue, head northeast on a flat section to Braintree Pass Path, then climb steeply up the south side of Chickatawbut Hill. The trail circles just south of the actual summit. Continue east over Fenno Hill and Kitchamakin Hill, then descend to Sassaman Notch. Climb up and over Nahanton Hill, then descend northeast over rolling terrain to Chickatawbut Road.

From Chickatawbut Road, climb northeast up and over Wampatuck Hill to a saddle, then climb up and over Rattlesnake Hill to Wampatuck

Road. From Wampatuck Road, follow the wide path across a causeway between St. Moritz Ponds to the eastern end of the trail at the parking lot for Shea Rink. From here, return the way you came or choose a new route back west.

NEARBY   South of Blue Hills on the other side of I-93/Rte. 128 (trail-head just south of exit 3), a 4-mile loop of mixed doubletrack trail and dirt road circles **Ponkapoag Pond** in Canton/Randolph. East of the pond, an overpass connects to a few trails east of Rte. 24.

DISTANCE 4 Miles **TOWN** Hingham
DIFFICULTY RATING Easy   **TRAIL STYLE** Loop
TRAIL TYPE Dirt Road **TOTAL ASCENT** 280 Feet

World's End is a spectacularly scenic, hilly coastal peninsula sticking north out into Hingham Harbor. It sits primarily on four glacial drumlin hills that are connected by lower saddles, cobble bars, or causeways. Between and among the hills are numerous wide-open fields and meadows. The rocky shoreline is nearly surrounded by the ocean or salt marsh (or both). Owned and managed by the Trustees, the reservation's manicured landscape features an appealing network of curving gravel carriage roads designed by the famous landscape architect Frederick Law Olmsted. In total there are 4.5 miles of trails, with numerous views out across Boston Harbor and to the Boston skyline in the distance. Most of the climbs rise at steady, gentle grades, and the footing is soft and gentle throughout; as such, this makes a terrific introduction to trail running for kids or beginners. There's an entrance fee for this very popular site, and both time and day reservations are required, but it's truly well worth the visit.

DIRECTIONS   From the rotary along Rte. 3A in Hingham, go east on Summer Street for 0.5 miles until it becomes Rockland Street at a 4-way intersection. Take a left onto Martin's Lane and go 0.7 miles north to the entrance gatehouse and bear right up to the dirt parking area. **GPS** "150 Martins Lane"

TRAIL   From the trailhead, follow the Weir River Road northeast, passing by several junctions with short side paths to the tidal marsh on the left. After passing over a small drainage channel and an unmarked path on the left, take a right onto the carriage path that leads to Rocky

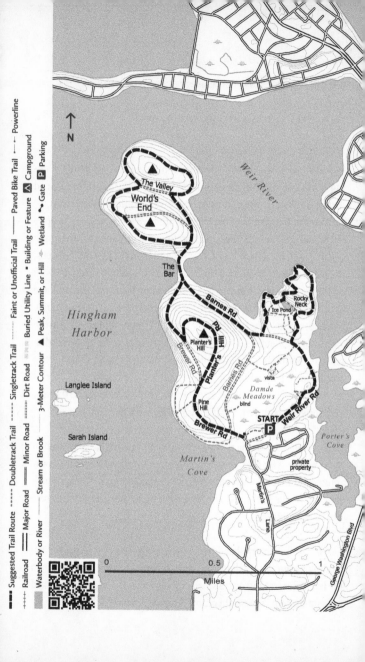

Legend

■■ Suggested Trail Route ----- Doubletrack Trail ----- Singletrack Trail ----- Faint or Unofficial Trail —— Paved Bike Trail +–+ Powerline
+++ Railroad —— Major Road ====== Minor Road ····· Dirt Road ▦▦ Buried Utility Line • Building or Feature ▲ Campground
—— Waterbody or River —— Stream or Brook —— 3-Meter Contour ▲ Peak, Summit, or Hill ⋆ Wetland ⌇ Gate 🅿 Parking

N ↑

The Valley
World's End
The Bar

Weir River

Barnes Rd
Rocky Neck
Ice Pond

Hingham Harbor

Planter's Hill
Planter's Hill Rd
Brewer Rd

Barnes Rd
vista
Damde Meadows
blind

Langlee Island

Pine Hill
Brewer Rd

START
🅿
Weir River Rd

Porter's Cove

Sarah Island

Martin's Cove

Martin's Lane

private property

George Washington Blvd

0   0.5   1
Miles

Neck. After passing two smaller paths leading uphill to the left, you'll reach Ice Pond on the left. Bearing right, continue on to Rocky Neck. Near the tip of this peninsula, the trail narrows. Follow the winding singletrack path counterclockwise back around to Ice Pond and return to Weir River Road the way you came in (or follow wooded singletrack/doubletrack paths that connect farther up Weir River Road).

Continue north on Weir River Road, heading slightly uphill. Very soon, bear right at a junction with Barnes Road. Go north, traversing the northeast side of Planters Hill, then descend to a junction at south end of a narrow, treeless spit called The Bar.

Cross the wide path over the top of The Bar, and then bear right at the next junction. This northern section of the property consists of three small loops over two of the drumlins that together are known as "World's End" proper. A small marshy saddle between the two hills is called The Valley. Running counterclockwise, stay right at all junctions until you return to The Bar (unless you choose to rack up extra mileage by making little loops over and around the hills). There's also a short, steep spur path leading down to the shoreline at the westernmost point of the peninsula.

From the southern end of The Bar, bear right on Brewer Road and go southwest up to a junction. Take a sharp left and climb Planters Hill, passing Brewer Grove along the way. At the top of Planters Hill, you'll find the Edwards Memorial at the end of a short side spur path.

Descend Planters Hill Loop back down to Brewer Road and keep heading south. You'll quickly cross over Pine Hill and then descend to a junction with Barnes Road. Stay straight, cross a wooden bridge over the mouth of the Damde Meadows tidal marsh (the open pool to the left), and return to the parking area.

NEARBY   On the east side of the scenic Weymouth Bock River estuary, Hingham's **Bare Cove Park** features a mix of paved trails, woodland paths, and gravel roads; on the west side of the cove, Weymouth's long and narrow **Great Esker Park** and adjacent **Osprey Overlook Park** offer a similar mix.

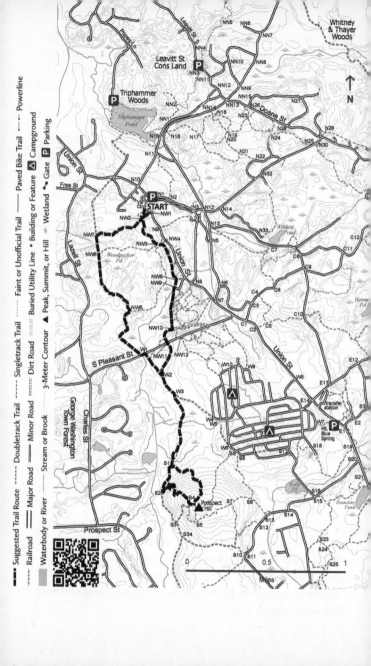

DISTANCE 4.4 Miles   **TOWN** Hingham
DIFFICULTY RATING Moderate   **TRAIL STYLE** Figure-8 Loop
TRAIL TYPE Singletrack/Doubletrack   **TOTAL ASCENT** 230 Feet

Wompatuck, or just "Wompy," features one of the largest and most diverse trail networks just south of Boston. It's laced with paved roads, dirt roads, and paved bike paths, but much of it is dirt singletrack and doubletrack trail, with occasional mountain-bike playground mazes. The site is also dotted with remnants of former naval usage, including concrete bunkers, rotting rail ties, mysterious fenced-off sections, and random old industrial doohickeys. Official park trails are blazed with blue directional markers on trees, and junctions/intersections are indicated with small lettered/numbered signs. This suggested route offers just a small sampling of the park's terrain and trail types; extension options are endless, and further exploration into the depths of the park can be very rewarding to the adventurous. Some parts feel very remote, and it's certainly possible to run all day here and never once retrace your steps.

DIRECTIONS   From Rte. 3, exit 35, take Rte. 228 north for about 4 miles. Turn right on Free Street and go 0.8 miles east to Lazell Street. Bear left on Lazell, then turn right on Union Street and go 0.4 miles east to Wompatuck Parking, on the left near the park Visitor Center. There are also entrances at the ends of Leavitt Street, Doane Street, and Mt. Blue Street, as well as at Whitney and Thayer Woods to the north.
GPS   "198 Union Street, Hingham"

TRAIL   From the NW1 junction sign just south of the Visitor Center, head southwest into the woods. Go straight at NW2 and continue southwest over rocky, rolling terrain to NW7. Turn left and go south on the wide, elevated rocky/grassy road. Continue straight at NW6 and pass Woodpecker Pond on the left. The trail soon curves left and narrows, then winds around a bit and crosses a boardwalk. Turn right at NW5 and follow rolling doubletrack over several more boardwalks. The trail swings left at a low spot and then parallels a fence on the right.

Turn left at the South Pleasant Street entrance, then quickly turn right at W1. Follow wide doubletrack up the hill to W2. Stay straight and continue southeast on an even wider road. Bear right at W3 and go due south on rolling doubletrack. Turn left at S1 and climb singletrack to S4. The wooded top of Prospect Hill (highest point in Hingham) is just to the left. Go right at S4 and descend swooping switchbacks to the bottom, then turn right at S2.

Head north, staying straight at S1 and W3, then bear right at W2 and descend to NW11. Cross South Pleasant Street and continue descending the wide, rocky path to an open area. Turn left at NW10 and head north along the right side of a stream; this stretch may be muddy. There is a warren of technical mountain bike trails and obstacles on the conifer-covered hillside to the right. Continue straight at NW9 and then bear left at NW8. Climb gradually up the hill, passing a concrete bunker on the right. Go straight across the intersection at NW4, then bear right at NW3. After passing another bunker, go straight at NW2 and then bear right to return to the Visitor Center.

NEARBY The Trustees' hilly **Whitney and Thayer Woods** property in Cohasset directly abuts Wompy to the north and offers an enjoyable mix of interconnected, easy-to-challenging doubletrack and singletrack trails as well as gravel roads. Cohasset's **Wheelwright Park** lies about a mile farther north; it and adjacent conservation properties feature a fun warren of rolling, well-signed trails. To the south, the small but scenic **Norris Reservation** in Norwell features several interesting loop trails.

DISTANCE 3.7 Miles   **TOWN** Abington

DIFFICULTY RATING Moderate   **TRAIL STYLE** Loop

TRAIL TYPE Singletrack/Doubletrack   **TOTAL ASCENT** 125 Feet

Ames Nowell State Park nearly rings Cleveland Pond. Although the majority of the park is flat, there are still many small hills, and roots and rocks are common throughout. Some of the lower-lying sections of trail are prone to flooding during wet times like early spring, especially around the northern tip of the lake. Markings and signage are sparse. The suggested route described here stays within park boundaries and samples a variety of terrain types. Mileage can easily be doubled or tripled by exploring the northwest part of the park or adding in extra loop options on the many unmarked singletrack trails and dirt roads running through the surrounding forest. The park is very popular with mountain bikers, who are responsible for much of the volunteer maintenance and upkeep of the trails.

DIRECTIONS From Rte. 3, exit 38B, go 6.4 miles south on Rte. 18 to Abington. Turn right on Randolph Street and go 0.1 miles. Turn left on Lincoln Street and go 1.1 mile. Turn left on Hancock Street and go 0.4 miles. Turn right on Presidential Drive and go 0.5 miles. Turn right on Linwood Street and go 0.1 miles north to the park entrance. Bear right at the ranger station and go 0.1 miles north to the large paved parking area on the left.

GPS "Ames Nowell Parking Area" or "724 Linwood Street"

TRAIL Starting at the northern end of the first (southern) parking area, take the red-blazed trail west through woods down toward the east shore of Cleveland Pond. Turn right at the first intersection and

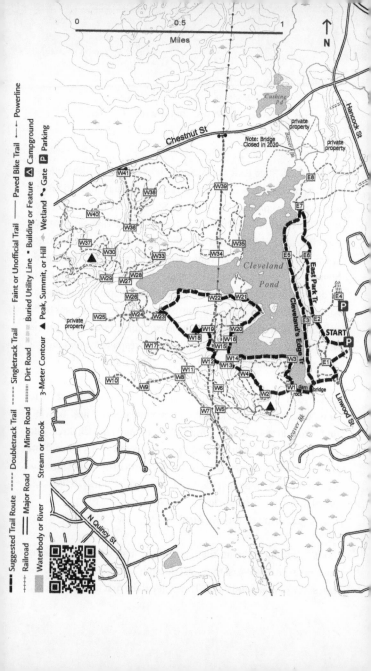

follow the doubletrack trail that runs north along the hillside above the pond. Stay straight at all junctions with trails that lead down the hill to the left (there are many). In about a half mile, you'll arrive at a lakeside picnic area near the north end of the lake.

At the picnic area, go left and follow the narrower trail along the edge of the lake, staying straight at all junctions with trails leading up to the left. This section is rooty and rocky, but very scenic and relatively flat. There are occasional blue markers.

At the south end of the lake, bear right and cross the pedestrian bridge just below the dam. Just past the large rock ledge, take the first right and follow the trail along the south shore of the lake. The width varies between singletrack and doubletrack. From W1, go north for 0.15 miles to W3, staying right at all junctions (except any short spurs leading to the water). From W3, follow the trail west along the south shore of the pond for 0.25 miles to W14, staying straight/right/west at several junctions/braids.

Go right at W14 and cross a marshy cove on a boardwalk to W16. Go right and continue northeast and then west for 0.3 miles to W21, staying straight at junctions and intersections with numerous trails leading right to the water and left up into the woods. From W21, go west. Cross a power-line swath and drop to a junction at W22. Continue west to W23.

Optional Extension   This junction makes a good starting point for a number of possible loop extensions in the northwest part of the park. Many of the paths there are winding, "flowy" mountain bike trails and are a lot of fun to run. Just watch for (and kindly yield to) bikes.

From W23, turn left and follow the doubletrack back toward the dam. Go straight at W18. Turn right at W19 and descend to W12. At W12, turn left and cross the power line to W13. Go straight and then bear right up the hill at an unmarked junction. Go straight at W4 and cross the top of the hill to W2 (there are a number of functionally parallel alternate singletrack options in this final section), then descend to W1 by the rock ledge just west of the dam.

Go east back across the dam at the south end of the pond. At an intersection, go either right or straight (both lead to the ranger station). From the ranger station, follow the road north back to the parking area.

> *Optional Extension*   Numerous loop options are possible in the southwest part of the park. To reach these trails, simply recross the dam and turn left at the big rock on the far side or just go straight west toward the power line and beyond. Some of them extend south into adjacent Beaver Brook Conservation Land.

NEARBY   Several miles north, trails of Braintree's **Cranberry Pond Conservation Area** and the abutting **Holbrook Town Forest** can be linked together for routes of up to 6 miles. Wildlands Trust's **Tucker Preserve** in Pembroke also has a small system of trails.

DISTANCE 9.5 Miles   **TOWNS** Easton and Sharon
DIFFICULTY RATING Moderate/Challenging   **TRAIL STYLE** Figure-8 Loop
TRAIL TYPE Singletrack/Doubletrack/Dirt Road   **TOTAL ASCENT** 450 Feet

The 1,800-acre Borderland park property offers over 20 miles of trails
in addition to other appealing features like scenic ponds, bare granite ledges, and a historic mansion (used as a filming location in the
movie *Knives Out*). There are many sections of soft, easy trail and an
equal amount of highly challenging technical stretches filled with
roots and rocks, especially in the twisty singletrack sections of the
northern half. All are runnable, save for the occasional stony patch
of "rock-garden" terrain. Looking closely, you may even discover a
hidden gem. The dominant forest of oak, pine, and beech is filled
with old stone walls, laced with bare granite ledges, and dotted with
giant boulders. The Bay Circuit Trail cuts north–south through the
park. There's a specifically designated off-leash zone for dogs here.

DIRECTIONS   From Mansfield, take Rte. 106 east for 2 miles. Turn
left on Stearns Avenue and go 1.2 miles. Turn left again on Mill Street
and go 0.7 miles. Turn left on Massapoag Avenue and go 1 mile north.
Turn right onto the park entrance road; the parking areas are on the
left. From Sharon, go south on Massapoag for 4.5 miles. Turn left
onto the park entrance road. Immediately bear left at a junction and
go 0.1 miles to a spacious paved parking lot.
GPS   "Borderland State Park, 259 Massapoag Avenue"

TRAIL   From the parking area, follow the wide, blue-blazed West
Side Trail north for 0.4 miles. Stay right where an unnamed trail
leads left. The footing alternates between smooth dirt and rough

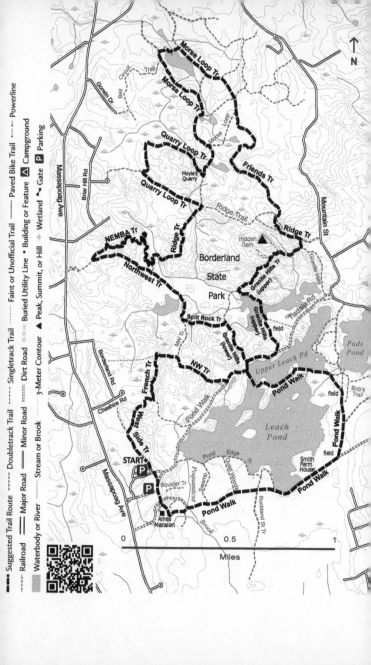

Legend

- ■ ■ Suggested Trail Route
- +++ Railroad
- ~ Waterbody or River
- ----- Faint or Unofficial Trail
- ——— Major Road
- ----- Doubletrack Trail
- ===== Minor Road
- ----- Singletrack Trail
- ::::: Dirt Road
- ----- Buried Utility Line
- ~ Stream or Brook
- —— Paved Bike Trail
- +—+ Powerline
- ■ Building or Feature
- ▲ Peak, Summit, or Hill
- 🌿 Wetland
- ⛺ Campground
- 🚪 Gate
- 🅿 Parking

Morse Loop Tr

Morse Loop Tr

Bay Circuit Trail

Gowin Dr

Quarry Loop Tr

Morse Loop

Friends Tr

Quarry Loop Tr

Moyle's Quarry

Briar Hill Rd

Ridge Trail

Ridge Tr

NEMBA Tr

Northwest Tr

Hidden Gem

Ridge Tr

Borderland

State

Park

Granite Hills Tr (upper)

Mountain St

Granite Hills (upper)

field

Tisdale Rd

Split Rock Tr

NW Tr

Granite Hills (lower)

Puds Pond

NW Tr

French Tr

Pond Walk

Upper Leach Pd

Bob's Trail

Cheshire Rd

West Side Tr

Pond Walk

Leach Pond

field

Borderland Rd

START

Boulder Tr

Pond Edge Tr

Lower Woods

Pond Walk

field

Ames Mansion

Pond Walk

Smith Farm House

Poquanticut Brook

Rockland St Tr

Massapoag Ave

↑ N

0   0.5   1

Miles

rocky patches. At a signed junction, turn left onto French Trail. This section coincides with the Bay Circuit Trail, with white circular BCT markers. Stay straight/right at several successive junctions with side trails leading left up to a bare rock ledge. In 0.3 miles, turn right onto Northwest Trail and descend, gradually at first and then more steeply down a set of broad steps. At the bottom, turn left on the wide Pond Walk road, following a sign pointing toward Mountain Street. After curving around a wetland to the right, stay straight at a junction. Soon after, turn left on Tisdale Road at an intersection where there's a view of Upper Leach Pond.

With the pond on the right, go north on Tisdale Road. At a junction, turn left on Granite Hills Lower Loop and climb 0.2 miles. Turn left on Split Rock Trail and go 0.2 miles west. There are several "split" rocks, though one in particular is about the size of a small house. Turn right on Northwest Trail and go 0.2 miles; several paths lead left to a view out over a wetland from a ledge. At a junction with Ridge Trail, continue straight/left on Northwest Trail for 0.3 miles, climbing gently to a junction.

Take a sharp right and follow NEMBA Trail 0.6 miles east. This winding singletrack is quite technical, with many roots and rocks. There are also several short braids in the trail along the way; stay right at each of them to run the coolest parts. The trail ends at a junction with Ridge Trail. Turn left on Ridge Trail and go 0.4 miles north to an intersection. This fun section rolls over and past a number of bare granite ledges.

Go left on Quarry Loop Trail and follow it for 0.7 miles, staying right at a junction with a trail leading left. This is an especially easy section of the route, with great footing the whole way. Pass by the mostly overgrown Moyle's Quarry on the right just before the end. At a junction, turn left and go 0.1 miles north. Then, at a junction with a bench, turn left on Morse Loop Trail and follow it for about a mile as it curves right around a pond, staying on the marked loop at all junctions (the BCT makes a sharp left at one). There's a nice vista at the pond's edge about halfway along, just past a braid in the trail.

Turn left on Friends Trail and go 0.7 miles, staying straight at a junction with a trail leading left and following occasional blue triangle markers. Early on, a long stretch of narrow boardwalk requires balance, and there is one patch of particularly stony rock garden terrain. You'll also play hopscotch with a stone wall for a bit. Near the bottom the trail braids; stay right to go up and over a bare granite ledge. Below the ledge, turn left on Ridge Trail and go 0.2 miles to a junction, again following a sign pointing toward Mountain Street. Next to a big boulder, go right on Ridge Trail. Soon after, turn left on Granite Ridge Trail (Upper Loop) and descend 0.4 miles, staying right at a bootleg trail junction.

Take a right on the wide Tisdale Road and follow it for 0.6 rolling miles along the north shore of Upper Leach Pond, staying straight at four trails leading to the right and then one short spur leading to the water's edge on the left. Back at the pinch point of the figure-8 loop, bear left and go 0.1 miles south to an intersection.

Turn left on Pond Walk and follow signs for about 1.6 mostly flat and smooth miles. After crossing the causeway between the two Leach Ponds, passing a wildlife viewing blind, then curving around to a junction with a trail to Pud's Pond on the left, the trail narrows slightly and emerges into open fields. Hug the right edge of the first field, cross through the middle of the next field, and bear right to follow the tree-lined dirt road through the final field. You'll pass a farmhouse and then one more wetland cove on the right. Return to the trailhead by following Pond Walk straight ahead to the Ames Mansion (bearing left at a junction just before the disc-golf course), then bearing right.

NEARBY Just north of Borderland, there are several miles of trail at **Inter Lochen Park** and **Rattlesnake Hill** in Sharon. The **Clifford G. Grant Reservation** in North Easton has a great 3-mile perimeter-loop trail that's flat and occasionally rocky, with numerous bridges and boardwalks. The **Bird Street Conservation Area** in Stoughton has a 5-mile loop with many smaller loop-option possibilities, though trails are unmarked and may be muddy or overgrown in parts.

DISTANCE 5 Miles **TOWN** Foxborough
DIFFICULTY RATING Moderate **TRAIL STYLE** Loop
TRAIL TYPE Singletrack/Doubletrack **TOTAL ASCENT** 430 Feet

This large site (sometimes just called Foxboro) is laced with all types of marked and unmarked trails and roads. This route sticks mostly to singletrack and doubletrack path, though there are many intersecting dirt roads and mountain-bike trails for easier and harder options. Some trails are blazed in only one direction, and navigation can be a significant challenge. Almost all of the trails are well drained, runnable, and worth exploring, though. There is no view from the actual high point, but Sunset Ledge offers a fine west-facing vista. This is a popular destination; if the main parking area is full, there are smaller access points at several of the gates around the perimeter of the property. Trails continue onto three adjacent properties: Wolf Meadow Area, Harold B. Clark Town Forest, and Cocasset Brook Greenbelt.

DIRECTIONS From, I-495, exit 36A, go north on Rte. 1 to the second intersection. Turn right on Thurston Street/West Street and follow signs to the state forest headquarters on Mill Street. There are parking lots on both sides of the street.

GPS "F. Gilbert Hills State Forest, 45 Mill Street"

TRAIL From the headquarters trailhead, follow the narrow, blue-blazed healthy-heart trail with the "hikers only" sign up into the woods (it's just to the right of Wolf Meadow Road). At a junction, go right on the wider Tupelo Trail and begin following green blazes. Stay left at a junction with Pine Hill Trail. Cross over Granite Street and then veer left and cross over Lakeview Road.

Just beyond the road, cross over a red-blazed trail and then follow

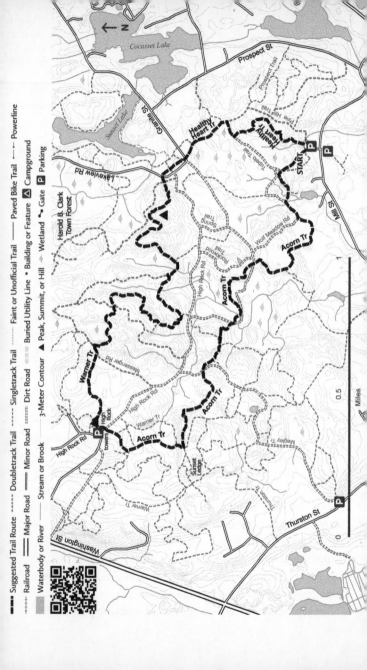

the green-blazed trail up into the woods. This great trail winds around a hill for a while before descending to a junction. Veering right, stay on the green trail and then turn left at a junction with the yellow-blazed trail (green and yellow together continue straight). Turn left and follow the yellow-blazed trail west to a junction.

Take a right onto an unblazed trail and climb up through a patch of large boulders. At the next unmarked junction, turn right and follow the trail up and down along the east side of a hill. The terrain is pretty rocky here. After climbing to an intersection, go straight and follow the yellow-blazed trail up the hill. At a junction with Messenger Road (unmarked), keep following the yellow blazes by going left and then right. A short distance up the hill pass a shelter, marking the midway point along the 33-mile Warner Trail. Keep climbing to High Rock at the top of the hill.

From High Rock, bear left and follow the white-blazed trail down to a parking area. Cross High Rock Road and keep the radio-tower-facility fence on your right. Stay straight where the white-blazed trail goes left and descend to an unmarked junction with Acorn Trail. Turn left and follow the magenta/pink-blazed Acorn Trail all the way back to the headquarters trailhead. Along the way you'll climb a restored stone staircase, decide whether to make an optional out-and-back to Sunset Ledge (you should), descend through several boulder fields, negotiate a few ledges, skirt a large wetland, and cross over Megley Trail and Wolf Meadow Road several times.

NEARBY **The Great Woods Conservation Area** in Mansfield has a decent network of trails. The town conservation areas of **Joe's Rock** and **Birchwold Farm** in Wrentham, along with **Mercy Woods** and **Diamond Hill Park** in northeast Rhode Island, offer a nice, nearly interconnected network of scenic trails. There's also a very dense trail tangle at **Wrentham State Forest**, but many are severely eroded, heavily used by off-road vehicles, poorly marked, uneven, overgrown, muddy, and not highly recommended for running. **Wheaton Farm** in Easton has a small system of fairly easy trails.

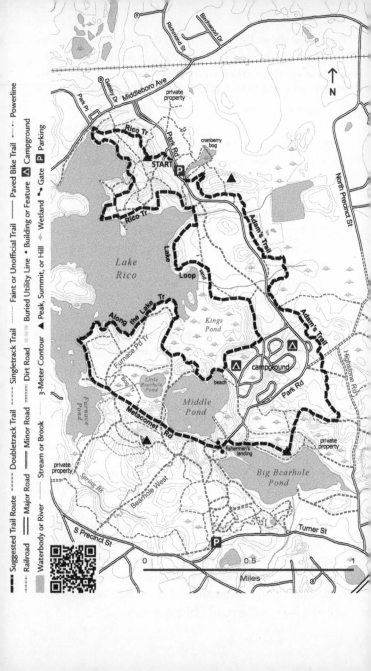

Legend

- ■ Suggested Trail Route
- ++++ Railroad
- ▓ Waterbody or River
- ----- Doubletrack Trail
- ── Major Road
- ── Stream or Brook
- ----- Singletrack Trail
- ──── Minor Road
- ----- Faint or Unofficial Trail
- ═══ Dirt Road
- ----- 3-Meter Contour
- ─┼─ Powerline
- ═══ Buried Utility Line
- ▲ Peak, Summit, or Hill
- ■ Building or Feature
- ◆ Wetland
- ▲ Campground
- ⌐ Gate
- P Parking
- ── Paved Bike Trail

N ↑

Richmond St
Birchwood Dr
Middleboro Ave
Gatsby Dr
Park Pl
Park Rd
Rico Tr
private property
cranberry bog
START
P
Rico Tr
Lake Rico
Lake Loop
pond
Adam's Trail
North Precinct St
Along the Lake Tr
Kings Pond
Furnace Pd Tr
Furnace Pond
Little Bearhole Pond
Bog Tr
campground
beach
Middle Pond
Park Rd
Highstone Rd
Metacomet Rd
fisherman's landing
Big Bearhole Pond
private property
private property
Spring Bk
Bearhole West
S Precinct St
Turner St
P

0   0.5   1
Miles

DISTANCE 6.5 Miles **TOWN** Taunton
DIFFICULTY RATING Moderate **TRAIL STYLE** Loop
TRAIL TYPE Singletrack/Doubletrack **TOTAL ASCENT** 340 Feet

Just a few miles from Taunton, Massasoit State Park includes a large, forested area of rolling hills and scenic ponds, laced with a dense network of more than 15 miles of dirt roads and trails of all types. Good trails for running include Rico Trail (white blazes), Lake Loop (no blazes), and Adams Trail (green blazes), as well as the park's many miles of doubletrack and unmarked singletrack. This loop route samples a variety of the park's terrain and trails. The unmarked trail leading north from the cranberry bog next to the parking lot is also very enjoyable.

DIRECTIONS From I-495, exit 14, go 0.5 miles south on Rte. 18. Turn right on Taunton Street/Middleboro Avenue and go 2.2 miles west. The park entrance will be on the left. Go 0.25 miles south to the first parking area.
GPS "Massasoit Park Road"

TRAIL On the northwest side of the parking area, look for the start of Rico Trail. Follow this white-blazed route up and over a hill. At a junction near the north side of Lake Rico (just south of Middleboro Avenue), turn left and follow Rico Trail south along the east side of the lake, rising and falling along the shoreline and staying on it at multiple intersections and junctions.

At a junction just after a steep drop and a bridge, turn right. Climb past a lookout and turn right on the Lake Loop trail. Follow this singletrack path south through the woods above the shore of the lake, staying right at all junctions. After passing an open sandy area, stay right and come out at the campground. Turn right on the campground road and follow it down to a building. Go right and follow the wide path across a dam next to Middle Pond. (Note that future trail reroutes are planned for the campground/dam area.)

From Middle Pond, bear right and enter the woods on an unmarked trail. Stay right at all junctions, with the marshy Kings Pond to your right, and eventually start tracing the south shore of Lake Rico. Following occasional blue blazes, follow the winding trail right next to the edge of the lake for about a mile around several coves and peninsulas. At a sign pointing to Five Ponds Trail, go right on the wide Metacomet Trail. Pass a sign for Bog Pond Trail on the left and proceed southeast to a gate along the paved Bearhole Road.

Optional Extension The south part of the park contains a dense network of mapped and unmapped singletrack trails, including several challenging ones on the steep sides of "Vulture Way" hill and a few flat and easy ones through a mostly flat pine grove to the east. All are flowy and fun to run, and many miles can be made up on them.

From a roadside platform (Fishermans Landing) overlooking Bearhole Pond, go north on Bearhole Road and immediately take a right toward an outdoor amphitheater. At the amphitheater, look for the southern end of the green-blazed Adams Trail. Take this trail 2 miles north back to the parking area, staying on it at all intersections and junctions (in several stretches the route is shared with a blue-blazed trail). There are several offshoots to the east, called the Front Nine and the Back Nine, that can make fun extensions.

NEARBY Several miles to the east, there are trail networks at **Pratt Farm** and **Rocky Gutter**. To the southeast, Betty's Neck Loop trail at **Lakeville Conservation Park** is about 3 miles total.

DISTANCE 4 Miles   **TOWN** Fall River
DIFFICULTY RATING Easy   **TRAIL STYLE** Loop
TRAIL TYPE Singletrack/Doubletrack   **TOTAL ASCENT** 110 Feet

Copicut Woods is a Trustees property anchoring the southern end of a vast forested area called Southeastern Massachusetts Bioreserve. The complex trail networks connect, but only the trails south of the Freetown/Fall River town line are closed to motorcycles, making this section more appealing for trail runners. Copicut's trails consist of a mix of singletrack, doubletrack, and old roads, many of which are lined with or pass through the elaborate stone walls of a long-abandoned farm. The trails are lightly marked but easy to follow, with map signs at many of the major junctions. *Copicut* is a Wampanoag word meaning "deep, dark woods," and that's precisely what you'll find and enjoy here.

DIRECTIONS   From Rte. 6 east of Fall River, take Sanford/Old Bedford Road 0.7 miles north. Turn left on Blossom Road and go 1.4 miles. Bear right on Indian Town Road and go 1.6 miles to the small parking lot on the left, marked by a Trustees sign.
GPS   "Copicut Woods Parking"

TRAIL   From the parking area, go northeast on Horseshoe Trail (just to the right of Brightman Trail) up into the woods. Early rocks soon give way to remarkably soft and smooth terrain underfoot. Cross over Yellow Hill Road, pass a gate, and continue northeast. The trail widens and curves right, eventually dropping south down to Indian Town Road.

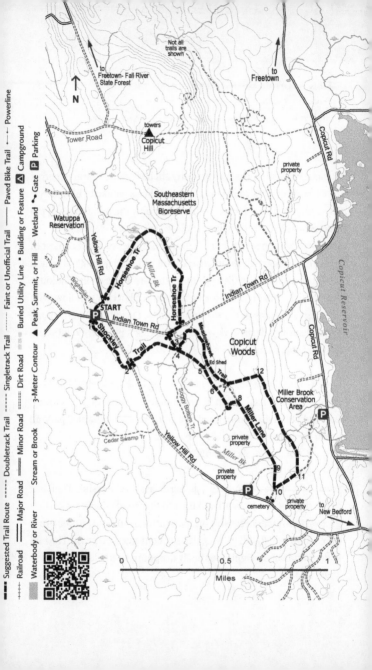

Optional Extension Shortly before Horseshoe Trail reaches Indian Town Road, a path leads left at junction (jct.) marker CH7 to a remote, mostly unmarked trail network in the central part of the Bioreserve. A fun and easy 2-mile lollipop loop can be made by taking this trail north (staying left at CH8 and CH9) to the first 4-way intersection (CH3) just below and to the east of 368-foot Copicut Hill, then taking rights at all turns, starting with CH2, back to the close of the loop portion at CH9. Note that several unmarked trails split off along the way, however, and navigation can be challenging.

Go right on the road, then turn left on Miller Lane. Descend to jct. 3, go straight, then turn left at jct. 4 onto Meadowhawk Trail. Follow the white-blazed trail east across Miller Brook, passing several unmarked paths leading left. Curving to the right, continue south to a covered picnic area.

Go southeast to intersection 7, then go left to jct. 12. Bear right and proceed at a more or less constant southeast bearing to jct. 11, crossing over Miller Brook again along the way. Go right and climb southwest up the wide grassy path to jct. 10.

Take a sharp right and go due north on the wide track of Miller Lane to jct. 9. Bear slightly left and head northwest in a straight line between imposing stone walls to jct. 8. Go left and follow the winding singletrack trail to a clearing at jct. 6, passing the currently closed Soggy Bottom Trail on the left.

Continue north, passing the impressive foundations of an old homestead, to jct. 5. Bear slightly left and go northwest to jct. 4. Just beyond, go left at jct. 3. Take the Shockley Trail northwest back to the parking area, passing over Indian Hill Road at intersection 2.

NEARBY To the north, **Freetown-Fall River State Forest** contains a maze of various multiuse trail types. One highlight is Assonet Ledge, an old quarry near the center of the property. Also look for "The Gem" trail north of Quanapoag Road. To the northwest, Fall River's

Watuppa Reservation directly connects to Copicut parking via the pleasant Brightman Trail and features several miles of wide trails. Just to the east of Copicut but not directly connected, there are several miles of trail at **Ridge Hill Reserve** in Dartmouth. West of Fall River, the dense trail network at **Village Park** in Swansea is terrific for trail running. To the south, you can combine the various colored-loop trails at **Destruction Brook Woods** in Dartmouth for an easy, nearly 10-mile run. Various trail loops at **Frank Knowles / Little River Reserve** in Dartmouth wind through scenic woodlands above Buzzards Bay; don't miss the impressive Boardwalk Trail across open salt marsh. **Dartmoor Farm / Slocum's River Reserve** also has nice trail loops. To the east, the roads and trails at The Bogs and Tripps Mill, both part of the **Mattapoisett River Reserve**, can be combined for an easy mid-distance run.

DISTANCE 4.4 Miles **TOWN** Duxbury

DIFFICULTY RATING Moderate **TRAIL STYLE** Loop

TRAIL TYPE Singletrack/Doubletrack **TOTAL ASCENT** 200 Feet

Comprising several conserved properties around North Hill Reservoir, North Hill Marsh Sanctuary is jointly managed by Mass Audubon and the town of Duxbury. Overall, the terrain is rolling and hilly, though some parts are flat and there are several active cranberry bogs scattered about. A network of trails and woods roads wind around Waiting Hill, Round Pond, Knapp Town Forest, O'Brien Bog, and more. This suggested route serves as a sampler of the various trail types, though many more miles can be added by exploring further.

DIRECTIONS From Rte. 3, exit 22, take Rte. 14 east for 0.2 miles, then turn right onto Lincoln Street, which becomes Mayflower Street. In about a mile, bear left. Parking is 0.5 miles ahead on the left; there's also a lot for Round Pond on the right.

GPS "North Hill Marsh, Mayflower Street"

TRAIL From the parking area, go north past the gate on the yellow-blazed fire road. In about 100 feet, bear left onto unmarked singletrack trail. This path gently swoops and rolls around the forested hillside. In about a half mile, cross over the wide yellow-blazed trail. Keep following the unmarked trail for another 0.35 miles to a complicated 5-way junction on the east side of an old bog, staying on it when it crosses other paths.

Briefly skirt the edge of the wetland, then bear right up into the woods, following the yellow blazes. Immediately bear left, then curve right where the yellow-blazed trail leads down to the left. The trail

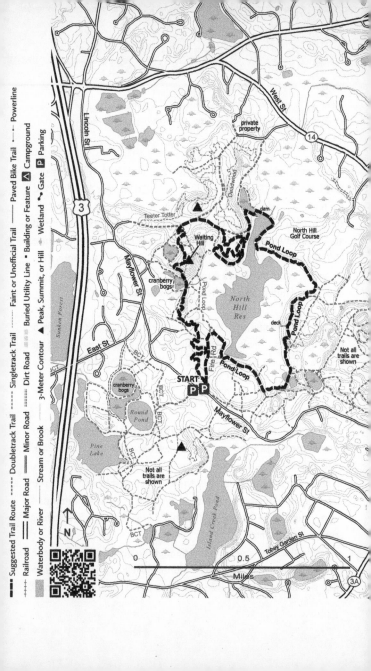

Legend

Suggested Trail Route ······ Doubletrack Trail ---- Singletrack Trail ······· Faint or Unofficial Trail ----- Paved Bike Trail ---- Powerline

++++++ Railroad ≡≡ Major Road ═══ Minor Road ▓▓▓ Dirt Road ░░░ Buried Utility Line ■ Building or Feature ▲ Campground

~~~~~ Waterbody or River ····· Stream or Brook ─── 3-Meter Contour ▲ Peak, Summit, or Hill 💧 Wetland ↖ Gate P Parking

N

0   0.5   1

Miles

climbs around the west side of Waiting Hill (unmarked side paths lead right over to the forested summit), then descends above east side of another bog. Turn right at a junction with a wide path at the bottom and go northeast a short distance to a 4-way intersection.

Optional Extension   At this point you can add on extra miles by taking a sharp left and going 0.2 miles west and then taking a right onto an unmarked trail called Teeter Totter (you'll see why before too long). This gorgeous singletrack path, along with one called Deadwood, winds crazily through the remote-feeling northern part of the site for 3 miles; it's rather complicated to follow but also extremely fun to run.

Go straight at the intersection, bear right at a fork, and then turn right onto unmarked singletrack. Take an immediate left and then wind around the hillside west of the pond. After descending gentle switchbacks, take two left turns and veer onto the blue-blazed Pond Loop Trail.

Now follow the more crowded, somewhat rooty, and often hilly Pond Loop clockwise nearly all the way around the pond, staying on it at all junctions. You'll pass a cranberry bog, cross an earthen dam, and skirt the edge of a golf course. Several short spur paths lead to pond views on the right. After curving right around the southern side of the pond, take a left off the blue trail on a dirt road by a pump house, then take another left and follow the yellow-blazed woods road back to the trailhead.

NEARBY   A wide connecting trail leads south through the woods to cranberry bogs at **Round Pond** and links up with the Bay Circuit Trail and paths around Pine Lake. About 10 miles west, several flat, easy loops can be strung together around the reservoirs of **Burrage Pond Wildlife Management Area** in Hanson/Halifax. To the north, there's a highly variable trail network at Marshfield's **Carolina Hill Reservation**.

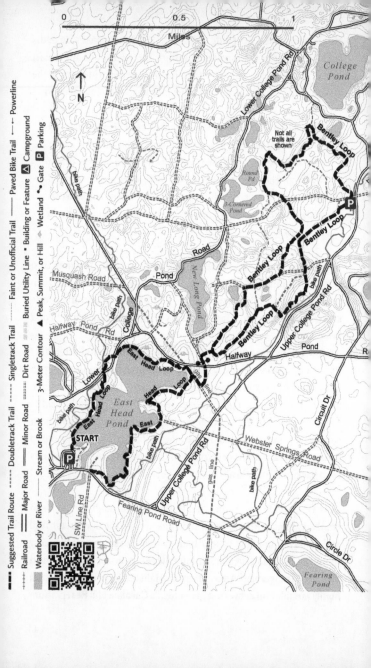

DISTANCE 6.7 Miles   **TOWNS** Plymouth and Carver
DIFFICULTY RATING Moderate   **TRAIL STYLE** Loop(s)
TRAIL TYPE Singletrack/Doubletrack   **TOTAL ASCENT** 330 Feet

Myles Standish State Forest is the largest public open space southeast of Boston. It is a vast area of dry, oak-pine-forest-covered, rolling sand-plain terrain pockmarked with frequent wetland depressions and ponds. The forest is laced with dirt roads, doubletrack-width hiking trails, and both mapped and unmapped singletrack trails. Some paved roads and bike paths pass though the property as well. The paths often rise and fall over the low hills, sometimes steeply. This route connects two primarily dirt singletrack and doubletrack trails in the central part of the forest, the East Head Loop (2.6 miles) and Bentley Loop (3.6 miles).

DIRECTIONS From I-495, exit 2, take Rte. 58 north for 2.5 miles. Go straight on Tremont Street for 0.8 miles. Turn right on Cranberry Road and go 2.7 miles east to the paved forest headquarters parking area.

From Rte. 3, exit 13 in Plymouth, take Long Pond Road about 4 miles south. Turn right on Alden Road and go 1.7 miles southeast. Bear left onto Upper College Pond Road and go 2 miles south (passing Parking Lot 2 on the right along the way). Turn right onto Halfway Pond/Lower College Pond Road and go 2 miles south.

GPS "194 Cranberry Road, Carver"

TRAIL Starting at the north end of the parking area, look for the Healthy Heart Trail marker near a potable water fountain and follow the somewhat unassuming trail into the woods. Just before East Head Pond, bear left at the first unmarked junction and begin following the trail clockwise around the pond's perimeter. Stay right at all junctions. The trail is not blazed but should be easy to follow, as it generally traces the western shoreline. There is a road crossing at 0.5 miles and another soon after.

At about 1 mile, just past a lengthy boardwalk section over a wet area, turn right at the open gas-line corridor and rise 0.1 miles to a junction. Turn left and follow the yellow-blazed Connector Trail to Bentley Loop, crossing over Halfway Pond Road and passing through gate B-2 along the way. Go north for a few hundred feet and then turn right at B-3. Still following yellow blazes, go a few hundred feet to a junction with the Bentley Loop at the edge of a clearing.

Go left and follow the blue-blazed Bentley Loop singletrack path in a clockwise direction. There are many junctions and intersections with marked and unmarked roads, trails, and paths along the way. The trail flows up and down numerous hills, passes wetlands/ponds, and traverses or skirts the edge of several grassy fields kept open for pheasant management. In about 2 miles you'll arrive at Parking Lot 2.

> *Optional Extension*   From Parking Lot 2, you can make a circuit on the 1.6-mile Frost Pocket Loop. Take the paved Frost Pocket Trail north for 0.6 miles. Turn right on Priscilla Road and descend 0.1 miles east. Turn right and follow the Frost Pocket Loop path south through several open barrens. This narrow, winding singletrack trail is steep and challenging. In 0.6 miles, go right on Three Corners Pond Road to climb 0.4 miles west back to Parking Lot 2.

From Parking Lot 2, continue following the blue-blazed Bentley Loop in a clockwise direction, again staying on it at all junctions and intersections along the way. Back at junction B-3, go left and follow the yellow-blazed connector trail back toward the East Head Loop Trail. At B-2, recross the road and follow the path back to the gas line. Turn right and follow the path a few hundred feet over to a junction.

Turn left and follow the unblazed East Head Loop Trail back to the headquarters parking lot. The trail hugs the eastern shoreline of East Head Pond and adjacent wetland coves, ending at a junction by the dam along Fearing Pond Road. Go right and follow the road back around to the parking lot.

Optional Extension About 2 miles southeast, the 4.8-mile Charge Pond Loop trail is accessible via the forest's paved bike-trail network. Total extra mileage from headquarters is about 9 miles.

NEARBY Just to the east, you can combine several trail loops at **Halfway Pond Conservation Area** in Plymouth. Several miles south, the 3.4-mile **Great Neck Trail** in Wareham makes a scenic, flat, easy lollipop-loop run if you combine the red and green loops; access from Crooked River Road. To the north, there are runnable public trail networks at **Plymouth Town Forest**, **Crawley Woodlands Preserve**, **Eel River Preserve**, **Foothills Preserve**, and **Black Cat Preserve** in Plymouth.

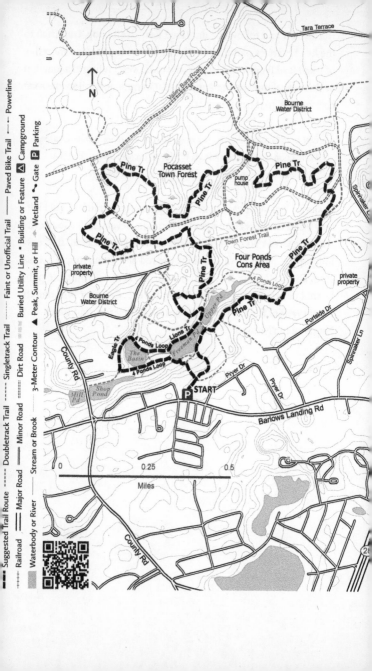

■ Suggested Trail Route ----- Faint or Unofficial Trail —— Paved Bike Trail ---- Powerline
+++++ Railroad ----- Singletrack Trail ----- Buried Utility Line • Building or Feature ▲ Campground
===== Doubletrack Trail —— Minor Road ===== 3-Meter Contour ▲ Peak, Summit, or Hill P Parking
■ Major Road ----- Dirt Road ~ Stream or Brook ≈ Wetland ⌐ Gate P Parking

Tara Terrace

Bourne
Water District

Pine Tr

Pocasset
Town Forest

Pine Tr

Pine Tr

pump
house

Pine Tr

Spinnaker L

Pine Tr

Town Forest Trail

Valley Bars Road

private
property

Four Ponds
Cons Area

Pine Tr

Pine Tr

private
property

Bourne
Water District

4 Ponds Loop

Unger Rd

Portside Dr

Pine Tr

Eagle Tr

4 Ponds Loop

Lions Tr

Freeman Rd

The Basin

4 Ponds Loop

Pyer Dr

Pyer Dr

Spinnaker Ln

Mill Pd

Shop
Pond

P START

County Rd

Barlows Landing Rd

0   0.25   0.5

Miles

County Rd

26

N

DISTANCE 4 Miles   **TOWN** Bourne
DIFFICULTY RATING Moderate   **TRAIL STYLE** Loop
TRAIL TYPE Singletrack   **TOTAL ASCENT** 225 Feet

Located in the Pocasset part of Bourne, Four Ponds Conservation Area features a very nice trail network centered around a string of scenic ponds and wetlands. The trails are shared with the adjacent Pocasset Town Forest to the north. Signage can be somewhat confusing, with several named trails (Lions, Eagle, and Town Forest) sharing segments or crisscrossing one another, especially right around the ponds, and some trail names not matching older maps. North of the more popular ponds part, however, the mostly gentle, well-marked 3.7-mile Pine Trail Loop quietly winds past hidden marshes and bogs in a gorgeous, rolling oak-pine-forest landscape. This lightly traveled section of trail is a real treasure and very fun to run.

DIRECTIONS From Rte. 28, take Barlows Landing Road 0.7 miles west to the small dirt parking lot on the right.
GPS "140 Barlows Landing Road, Pocasset"

TRAIL Starting at the trailhead, follow the entrance path north into the woods. At the first junction, turn left and follow 4 Ponds Loop down the rooty hillside. Take two lefts and then briefly trace the shore of Freeman Pond. Crossing several wooden bridges, stay left where two "cross-connector" trails lead across narrow land strips between ponds/wetlands on the right, then turn right at a grassy area by Shop Pond. Follow "4 Ponds Loop" signs along the north shore of Turtle Pond/The Basin, Freeman Pond, and Upper Pond, ignoring several steep, unmarked trails leading left and three connector trails on the right.

At a wooden post, turn left and start following the circular black-arrow markers of the Pine Trail. After climbing a short hill, the initially wide trail swings right and joins another wide path. Go 0.1 miles north, then turn right onto a narrow singletrack path that immediately starts winding back and forth through the woods.

Follow the black arrows and signs of the highly runnable Pine Trail for the next 2.5 miles as it meanders around and over low hills. The soft surface is mostly packed sand and dirt, with occasional rocks and roots. You'll cross directly over numerous other trails, grassy lanes, and dirt roads and pass a pumping station shack about halfway along. Stay on the marked trail at all junctions/intersections.

Pine Trail eventually links up with 4 Ponds Loop again, and the two coincide for a stretch. Follow the markings southwest above the south shore of Freeman Pond. Pass an unmarked path leading up to the left, then pass a trail with a sign pointing to the parking lot. Take a left at a second "Parking Lot" sign and follow the wide path back to the trailhead.

NEARBY Several miles south, **Frances Crane WMA** is notable for its wide expanses of open sandplain meadows east of the railroad tracks where the trails are mostly doubletrack and dirt roads. A dense maze of excellent, hilly, unmarked singletrack paths lace the oak-pine woods west of the tracks. Footing is mostly smooth, but there are a number of rough sections and a few steep pitches. A rolling, sometimes-grassy 3.5-mile woods road circles **Long Pond** reservoir in Falmouth, while several shorter, narrower paths loop around adjacent wetlands. The 9-mile **Moraine Trail** connects Frances Crane and Long Pond, with numerous side trails, bogs and vernal pools, and hilltop vistas of Buzzards Bay along the way. **Beebe Woods** and neighboring **Peterson Farm** in Falmouth feature a combined network of 6–7 miles of old roads and foot trails; access from parking at the end of Highfield Drive. Loop options at **Coonamessett Bogs** (Falmouth), **Quashnet Woods** (East Falmouth), and **Long River Trail** (Mashpee) all make good 3- to 4-mile riverside runs.

DISTANCE 5 Miles **TOWN** Barnstable
DIFFICULTY RATING Moderate/Challenging **TRAIL STYLE** Loop
TRAIL TYPE Singletrack **TOTAL ASCENT** 270 Feet

This popular town-owned/maintained area (formerly called Trail of Tears, or ToT) offers more than 20 miles of winding trails for pedestrians and bikers, as well as a number of wider fire roads. There are many small hills and a handful of higher ones; the singletrack trails shoot up and down them as often as possible. The property is more or less bisected once by an east–west power-line swath and again by the north–south-oriented Crocker Road, resulting in four general quadrants. The suggested route explores a sampling of the site's features and terrain types, but extension options are plentiful and well worth investigating.

DIRECTIONS From Rte. 6, exit 65, go 0.8 miles south on Rte. 149/ Prospect Street, then turn right on Popple Bottom Road. The small parking area is on the right. Alternate parking can be found on the south side of the property at 1590 Race Lane in Marstons Mills and in the northeast corner at a parking lot where power lines cross Service Road.

GPS "West Barnstable Conservation Area, Popple Bottom Road"

TRAIL From the trailhead at P3, head north up the hill on Briar Ridge Trail. Curving left, pass a closed path on the right and then cross over the wide Popple Bottom Road at E11. Continue west and south down the hill. At SE9, turn right and go northwest on Danforth Trails. Continue straight at SE8 and continue northwest on Danforth Bypass. Turn left at SE7 and go northwest on Airport Trail. It braids before long; take the slightly longer left option and then bear left when

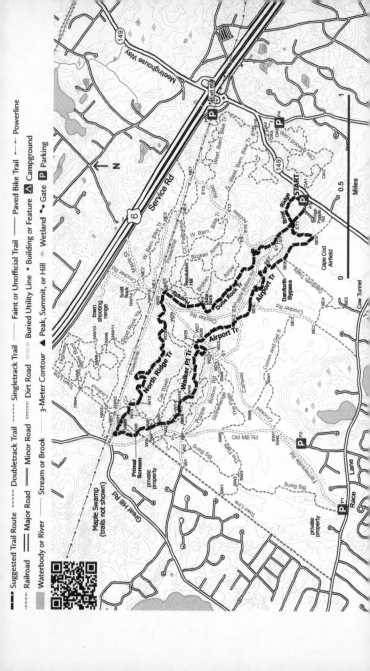

they rejoin. Still trending northwest, cross Crocker Road at SE6, then Popple Bottom Road at E2, and then Crooked Cartway at W26.

Just past W26, turn left onto Walker Point Trail at W25. Stay on this trail all the way up to a deck with a view at Walker Point by turning right at W23, then bearing left at W18, W16, and W14.

From Walker Point, head north-northwest on a gently rolling single-track path. Bear right at an unmarked fork, then cross over a narrow lane of pavement. At W8, continue northwest on Primal Scream. This trail braids, and you can choose either branch; both are sweet. Just past where the paths rejoin, take a sharp right and climb to a vista called "The Lookout" at the highest point in Barnstable (232 feet) at W11.

From The Lookout, head southeast on the roller-coastery, gradually descending North Ridge Trail. To follow this trail, stay straight at W13, bear left at an unmarked junction with No Brakes on the right, and then stay straight/right at W15 where a trail leads left over to the power lines. After winding around the ridge and dropping elevation, bear left at W28 and then cross over Crocker Road at W30.

At W5, turn right on Humpty and go south, keeping a meadow ("Field of Dreams") on your left. Pass a boulder called Dube Rock at E4, then bear right and start following Dube Rock Trail southeast. At E7, bear left onto the wide Popple Bottom Road and follow it all the way back to the trailhead, staying straight at E7, E9, and E11.

Optional Extension(s)   There are numerous other fun possibilities at WBCA. A few notable ones:

1. The red-blazed West Barnstable Biking Trail loop just northeast of this one is a challenging 3- to 4-mile route. It is very hilly and occasionally tough to follow (it braids quite a few times), but still fun to run. It can be linked to directly or easily accessed from the service-road parking lot under the power lines.

2. Broken Arrow is a short, hilly loop sandwiched in between the suggested route and the Biking Trail mentioned above.

3. The 1.5-mile Otis Atwood Loop just east of Rte. 149 is another hilly, curvy option.

4. A warren of trails north of the power lines in the northwest section features more hilly and very curvy options.

5. A handful of fun trails generally parallel Walker Point Trail, including Stonehenge, Tractor Tire Trail, Three Witches, and Car Wash.

6. Trails in the southern section are flatter and pass by open meadows (with beautiful wildflower blooms in season); these can be accessed from an official parking area at 1590 Race Lane.

NEARBY Immediately to the west, a similar large tangle of trails threads through the very hilly **Maple Swamp Conservation Area** in Sandwich; the Jacob's Ladder Trail and Sam Nyes Mtn. vicinities are especially enjoyable there. Several miles east, the convoluted path

Jacob's Ladder Trail at Maple Swamp Conservation Area in Sandwich.

complex at **Hyannis Ponds WMA** is entirely unmarked, but intrepid explorers can find plenty of exciting singletrack there, ranging from gentle rolling undulations to steep technical hills; search for fun trails known as The Back Nine, Bushwood, Burning Man, Automile, and The Wall; parking is very limited. **Horse Pond Conservation Land** in West Yarmouth has a small system of mostly easy trails. The **Bud Carter Conservation Area** in Yarmouth features a network of footpaths with lots of little ups and downs throughout; parking is limited.

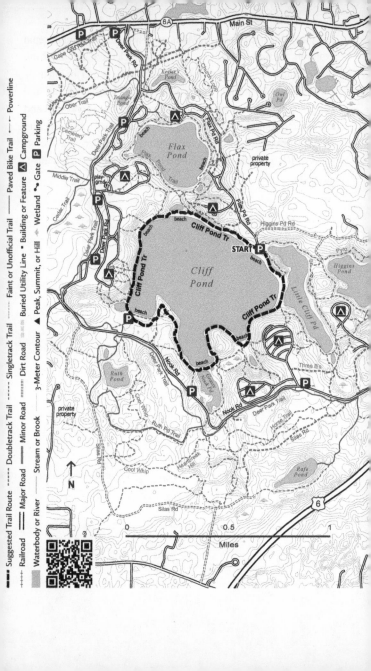

DISTANCE 3 Miles **TOWN** Brewster
DIFFICULTY RATING Moderate **TRAIL STYLE** Loop
TRAIL TYPE Singletrack **TOTAL ASCENT** 90 Feet

Located near the middle of Cape Cod, Nickerson State Park is laced with hiking trails, paved bike paths, and campground roads and features eight named kettle ponds, many of which are ringed with clean sandy beaches. The simple route described here circles the park's largest pond but represents just a fraction of its sandy, rock-free singletrack trails; there are many more threaded throughout, both mapped and unmapped. The path occasionally gets a little narrow and the ponds are very popular, so watch out for other users. Other good loops include Little Cliff Pond Path (1.4 miles), Flax Pond Path (1.4 somewhat-rugged miles), and Higgins Pond (1.1 miles), as well as combinations of any of the less traveled upland forest paths and mountain-bike trails. The trails at Nickerson are surprisingly hilly, but most of the climbs are relatively short. Bikes are not allowed on the paths around the ponds.

DIRECTIONS From Rte. 6, exit 89 in Orleans, take Rte. 6A west for about 1.5 miles to the main park entrance. Turn left on Deer Park Road and go 0.4 miles south. Turn left on Flax Pond Road and go 1 mile southeast to the small Cliff Pond Beach parking area at the end. There are several alternate parking options.
GPS "Nickerson State Park"

TRAIL Starting at the parking area, head west into the woods on the yellow-blazed Cliff Pond Trail and begin following it counterclockwise around the edge of the pond. Stay left at all junctions for the entire loop, ignoring all side trails leading upslope to the right. After navigating a fairly eroded section (the first of several on this loop), you'll arrive at an open sandy beach on the north side of the pond.

The trail blazes start again in the pines at the far side of the beach. Pass by several large boulders at the water's edge, then navigate a narrow tunnel of vegetation along the western shore of the pond until you arrive at a junction just below Firetower Hill. Bear left and pass between the main pond and a smaller one on the right and then arrive at another open beach.

The trail reenters the woods slightly uphill from the water's edge, climbs briefly, and then drops back to the pond. The next section is especially enjoyable as the trail winds around a couple of peninsulas on the south side of the pond and roller-coasters up and down a number of hills. Short beach sections line the coves in between.

On the east shore of the pond, the trail runs north along an isthmus between Cliff Pond and Little Cliff Pond. You can add extra miles by looping around Little Cliff Pond (and Higgins Pond). After passing several boat-rental houses on the beaches, continue following the path along the northeast shore to return to the trailhead.

Optional Extensions   A particularly runnable section of unmarked singletrack trail gently rises 1.25 miles south from just west of the Old Cemetery sign on the paved Ober Trail bike path up to Middle Trail. Other unpaved singletrack trails that are good for running at Nickerson include Bomber Trail and Firetower Hill in the west part; Church and Take-Me-To-Church in the north part; Pyro, Higgins Hill, Skinny Trail, Do-the-Dew, and The Race in the east; and Cool Whip, Heartbreak Hill, and Horse Race in the south. There are also numerous doubletrack trails, fire roads, paved bike paths, and paved roads within the park.

NEARBY   There is a network of unmarked singletrack trails just south of Freemans Way, including the 4-mile Training Loop; these paths—as well as fun, uncrowded singletrack loops south of Ruth Pond—are accessible from **Brewster Recreational Park**. Several miles to the west, you can combine various color-coded loop trails at **Punkhorn Parklands** between Upper Mill Pond and Seymour Pond in Brewster. Additionally, bayside beaches in the Brewster area are magnificent for running; check out Breakwater, Linnell, and Crosby Landing beaches. There is also a small, scenic trail system at **Bell's Neck Conservation Lands** in Harwich.

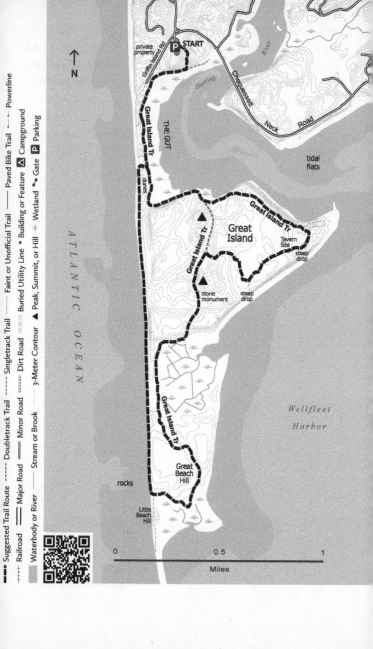

Suggested Trail Route ■■■ **Doubletrack Trail** ----- **Singletrack Trail** ...... **Faint or Unofficial Trail** ----- **Paved Bike Trail** ----- **Powerline**

++++ **Railroad** ━━━ **Major Road** ━━━ **Minor Road** ====== **Dirt Road** ▩▩▩ **Buried Utility Line** • **Building or Feature** 🅰 **Campground**

━━━ **Stream or Brook** ━━━ **Waterbody or River** ━━━ **3-Meter Contour** ▲ **Peak, Summit, or Hill** ☀ **Wetland** ☛ **Gate** 🅿 **Parking**

↑ N

private property

🅿 **START**

Griffin Island Rd

Herring River

Chequessett

Neck

Road

tidal flats

THE GUT

Great Island Tr

dunes

Great Island Tr

Great Island

Tavern Site

steep drop

Great Island Tr

🅰

🅰

stone monument

steep drop

ATLANTIC OCEAN

Wellfleet Harbor

Great Island Tr

Great Beach Hill

Little Beach Hill

rocks

0   0.5   1

Miles

DISTANCE 6.5 miles   TOWN Wellfleet

DIFFICULTY RATING Moderate   TRAIL STYLE Lollipop Loop

TRAIL TYPE Singletrack/Doubletrack   TOTAL ASCENT 270 Feet

There are a handful of hikes in Massachusetts that can legitimately be called epic adventures; the sandy trail out onto Great Island is one of them, and it makes a really fun run. Highlights of this wild seacoast route include vistas across open salt marshes, lofty dunes, long stretches of sandy beach, and views from the pitch-pine-forest-covered heights of Great Island and Great Beach Hill. Optional extensions lead to the site of a colonial-era tavern and out onto tidal spits. Timing is a major factor in this trek, and some portions along the salt marsh may be impassable at high tide, especially at the southern tip; consult current tide charts before setting out. Pets are not allowed south of the first cut, and parts of the upper beach and dunes may be closed for shorebird nesting during parts of the spring and summer.

DIRECTIONS From Wellfleet Center just west of Rte. 6, take Chequessett Neck Road 2.5 miles west to the spacious, paved Great Island parking area on the left (about 0.3 miles after crossing a causeway over Herring River).

GPS "Great Island Trail, 2 Griffins Island Road, Wellfleet"

TRAIL From the trailhead on the east side of the parking area, follow the gravel path of Great Island Trail south through the woods and down log steps to a tidal marsh. Turn right and follow the upper edge of the marsh west (this stretch may be tricky at very high tide). Staying on the trail as it curves left/south, pass by several unmarked paths leading upslope on the right and arrive at a narrow isthmus of sandy dunes between Cape Cod Bay to the west and a section of marsh called "The Gut" to the east.

Heading south, cross the isthmus by staying along the upper edge of the bay left of the dunes. The trail braids a few times; all strands are scenic, but which one you choose may depend on the tide. When you reach Great Island (technically not an island anymore), bear left and follow the trail along the edge of the bay below the forest. At a small cove, the main trail climbs up into the forest and crosses over the middle of the island; bear left here onto a narrow path leading along the upper edge of the marsh edge. Follow this path up into the pine forest and then down to the eastern tip of the island. Curving right, continue past the former site of a colonial-era tavern (now just a small pile of rocks). You'll also pass two short spurs on the left to overlooks atop steep bluffs above Wellfleet Harbor. Take a left back at the wide north–south cart path that cuts across the middle of the island and continue south on the main trail to a second isthmus.

Go south between the marsh on the left and the dunes on the right to Great Beach Hill, passing a short link trail to the beach on the right. Bearing slightly left, climb a short sandy pitch and then follow the trail into uplands on the island. A spur path leads to Jeremy Point Overlook. The trail then descends to the marsh edge, curves right, and heads west to the main beach. To the south, the Jeremy Point sandbar is submerged at high tide and should be explored only at the lowest tides.

Go right and head north on the beach with the ocean to your left. This stretch—which isn't really a trail but should be very easy to follow—is entirely exposed and out in the open; the soft sand may be challenging to run in. About two-thirds of the way up the isthmus north of Great Island, take a right through a break in the dunes to close the loop. Return to the trailhead the way you came or take the wooden-fence-lined side path left up to Chequessett Neck Road and then go right on the road.

NEARBY   The **Nauset Marsh Trail** in Eastham is a scenic, 1.3-mile loop partly along a salt pond; portions are sandy and rooty, but it is easy overall. A "minimally maintained" path out to **Coast Guard Beach** adds an extra 2 miles round-trip. These trails cross or coincide with a busy paved bike trail in places. Pets are not allowed.

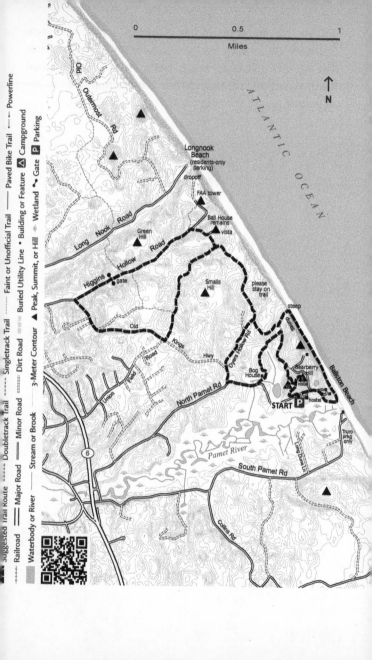

DISTANCE 6.3 Miles **TOWN** Truro

DIFFICULTY RATING Easy/Moderate **TRAIL STYLE** Loop(s)

TRAIL TYPE Singletrack/Doubletrack/Dirt Road **TOTAL ASCENT** 440 Feet

Just north of the Pamet River, sandy trails and fire roads wend through coastal oak and pine forests in a secluded part of Cape Cod National Seashore. The dynamic landscape features rolling hills, wild coastline, and a tidal river that bisects this 3-mile-wide section of the Cape. Highlights awaiting adventurous trail runners here include the twin summits of Bearberry Hill, where there are spectacular views of Ballston Beach and old cranberry bogs, the remains of a cranberry "Bog House," forest solitude, and isolated beaches. This route consists of two "lobes" and is relatively moderate and easy to follow overall, despite multiple junctions and intersections. Pets are not allowed.

DIRECTIONS   From Rte. 6, take the Pamet Roads–Truro Center exit. Turn left on North Pamet Road and go 1.6 miles to the Hosteling International Truro Hostel at the old Coast Guard Station near Ballston Beach (valid beach stickers are required to park along North Pamet Road). Turn right onto the hostel driveway and then take an immediate right into a small free parking area with room for about ten vehicles (parking is limited to two hours). Do not park in the hostel lot. There is no public restroom or water available at the parking area or the hostel.

GPS "HI Truro Hostel, N Pamet Road"

TRAIL   Take the short path north from the National Seashore trail map at the northwest corner of the parking area, avoiding the dense poison-ivy patch bordering the lot. Carefully cross North Pamet Road to the opening in the split-rail fence. Immediately bear left on the obvious and well-used sandy path, paralleling the road at first, and then curve north up into the woods. At an intersection, go right and climb to the open eastern summit of Bearberry Hill for unsurpassed views of the beach, the ocean, and the marshy head of the tidal Pamet River. Descend back to the intersection and go straight on the narrow path up Bearberry Hill West. At the top, an educational placard describes the Outer Cape's cranberry-harvesting history. Catch a glimpse of the shingled Bog House roof in the cranberry-bog depression below.

Head back down to the intersection and take the trail to the left to descend the north side of the hills. Navigate several wooden water bars and pass through a dry pitch-pine forest before encountering a T-junction with a wider path (a small "Trail" signpost points left). Turn left and go north to a four-way trail intersection. You'll return to this spot later, but for now take a sharp left on a narrow trail. Bearing left at the only fork, go about a half mile south/southwest to the remains of the Bog House. From the building, head southwest on grassy doubletrack fire road to North Pamet Road.

Turn right and follow the paved road uphill for about 0.25 miles, being mindful of blind corners and traffic. Turn right onto Old Kings Highway, a gravel road, and go a short way north to a fork. Bear right on Dyers Hollow Road. At 0.4 miles from North Pamet, after passing a private residence on the right, take the path leading up to the right from the road. Soon after, turn left onto a pristine piece of singletrack. Passing several faint trails on the right that lead to views of the Atlantic, gently ascend through a dense woodland to an obvious Y-junction in about a half mile. Bear left/southwest and follow gently rolling singletrack trail through the coastal forest below Smalls Hill on the left. In 0.7 miles, pass through two waist-high metal pylons and go right on a sandy stretch of Old Kings Highway. Curving right, rise gently, eventually (legally) passing between a home and well-kept garden. Then descend to a junction with the paved Higgins Hollow Road and turn right. In 0.2 miles it turns to a gravel fire road.

Optional Extension   To add an extra 4 or more miles to the run and bump up the difficulty level, you can do a northern lollipop loop. It requires more attention to navigation but features serene paths and amazing views. About 0.1 miles east from the start of the gravel fire road, turn left on the technical singletrack trail; this special section is fun to run in both directions. In 0.3 miles, go right on Longnook Road, then look for a path on the left at the split-rail fence about 40 meters ahead. Climb a very steep hill, then go north for almost a quarter mile to a fork. From here, you can make a somewhat complicated loop by combining the trail heading north, Old Outermost Road, Old Kings Highway, and portions of other dirt roads, broken paved roads, and narrow singletrack paths south of the Highlands Center.

Continue east on Higgins Hollow Road until it ends at a chained-off asphalt road after 0.5 miles (there's a white aviation tower at the top of that hill). Bearing right, take the broken asphalt ribbon southeast up a short but sustained climb to the ruins of the old Ball House and a wooden bench with views of the Atlantic. On the ascent, note the singletrack trail coming in on the right about halfway up. From the top, head back to the singletrack, go left, and descend a short hill to a junction that closes the northern loop. Continue straight for a half mile, gradually descending to the intersection with the path to the Bog House. Here, take the sand trail heading sharply left/east into the dunes and beach grasses. Staying on the established path, climb a short, sandy pitch, then descend steeply on the other side. Turn right at the ocean and run south along the beach, with eroding dune bluffs towering above you on the right (this section may be unnerving at high tide). In about a half mile, go right at an established entrance/exit and climb up through a gap in the dunes. The sand gives way to the broken asphalt of North Pamet Road; the hostel will be on the left.

NEARBY   Patchwork fire roads and both official and unofficial single-track paths abound in Truro and Wellfleet, particularly in the Wellfleet ponds and **Newcomb Hollow** vicinity to the south (though parking can be a significant challenge there) and in the **Head of the Meadow Beach / Pilgrim Heights** area to the north. The wild **Dune Shacks Trail** in Provincetown is an unmarked excursion across open sand dunes to the beach beyond; the trek is about 2.5 miles round-trip, but it can be extended as long as you like by running along the beach. Make sure to bring water on this adventure.

Ballston Beach and Pamet Hollow from the windswept summit of Bearberry Hill (east peak) in Truro.

Massachusetts's two largest and most-populated islands require extra effort (and money) for visitors to get to, but nevertheless reward runners with a number of terrific trail sites.

Martha's Vineyard

The **Menemsha Hills Reservation** in the southwest part of Martha's Vineyard features a network of marked, rolling loop trails that pass near the island's second highest point, include numerous scenic viewpoints, and even lead down to the windswept edge of the ocean. The easy to moderate trails pass through a variety of coastal landscapes and environments. In general, the land slopes westward down toward the ocean, so the return to the trailhead includes more climbing. Poison ivy is abundant. Bikes are not allowed.

Manuel F. Correllus State Forest, located right in the middle of the island, features about 14 miles of sandy paths, trails, and fire roads over mostly flat terrain and offers summer runners a quiet break from the more crowded towns and villages. Though the shade is nice, the oak woodlands habitat can be hot and dry at times; bring plenty of water with you. Beware that there is also a lot of poison ivy around. From the parking lot at Riverhead Field on Barnes Road, an easy loop can be made by combining Dr. Fisher Trail (1.5 miles), Quampache Path (1.5 miles), and Red Trail (about 1 mile). Several unofficial trails and loops intersect established routes throughout the forest.

About two miles west of Edgartown, combine the purple trail and the yellow-blazed Garrett Family Trail at the **Caroline Tuthill Wildlife Preserve** for a circuitous but pleasant, easy, short (about 2.5 miles), and relatively uncrowded run. Many of the island's beautiful beaches are also great for anyone looking to run right along the water; **South Beach** on the southeast side is mostly rock free, and you can run uninterrupted for miles.

Nantucket

Middle Moors is the largest undeveloped open-space area on Nantucket, consisting primarily of shrubland but with some open heathland and grassland and a little bit of forest. The site is laced with a well-maintained patchwork of paths, trails, and roads that are well used by runners looking to get off paved roads. It serves as the cross-country course for the local high school, and an annual 5K race benefiting the Nantucket Conservation Foundation is held there. A relatively easy 6-mile loop run visits a variety of natural features like kettlehole ponds, a glacial erratic boulder, and the eponymous moors. Aside from the half-mile out-and-back access trail at the start/end, the route consists of two sections: an open southern loop of just under 3 miles around Milestone Cranberry Bog (an active commercial cranberry wetland) and a northern loop of about 2 miles, mostly through woodland and shrubland habitat, that visits Altar Rock, the fourth-highest point on the island.

About two miles west of the village lies Nantucket's other great trail-running site: **Nanahuma's Neck**. Encompassing Sanford Farm, Ram Pasture, and The Woods properties, it features a network of rolling, sandy trails through woodlands, shrub thickets, and grasslands. From the Medaket Road trailhead, take the 6-mile Ocean Walk loop all the way to the beach at the island's southern shore.